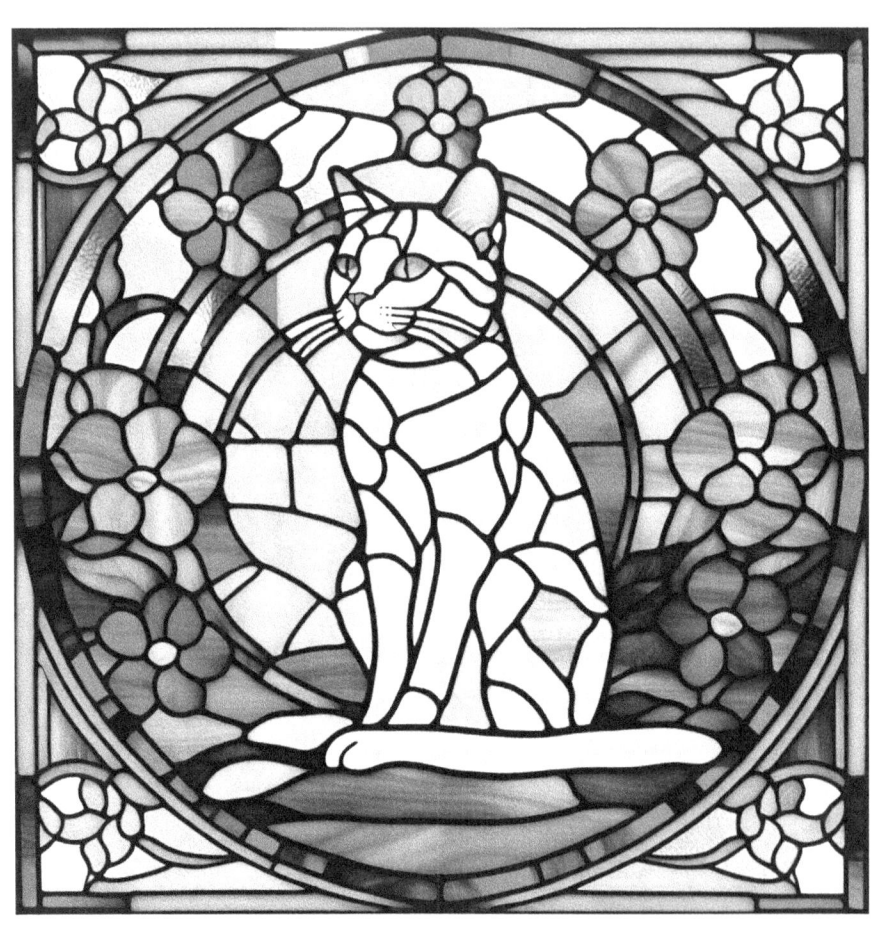

FOR KITTY, FRANCIS & KASI & MAUSI

KDB-ISBN: 9798864468081

IMPRINT: INDEPENDENTLY PUBLISHED
HERSTELLUNG AMAZON DISTRIBUTION GMBH

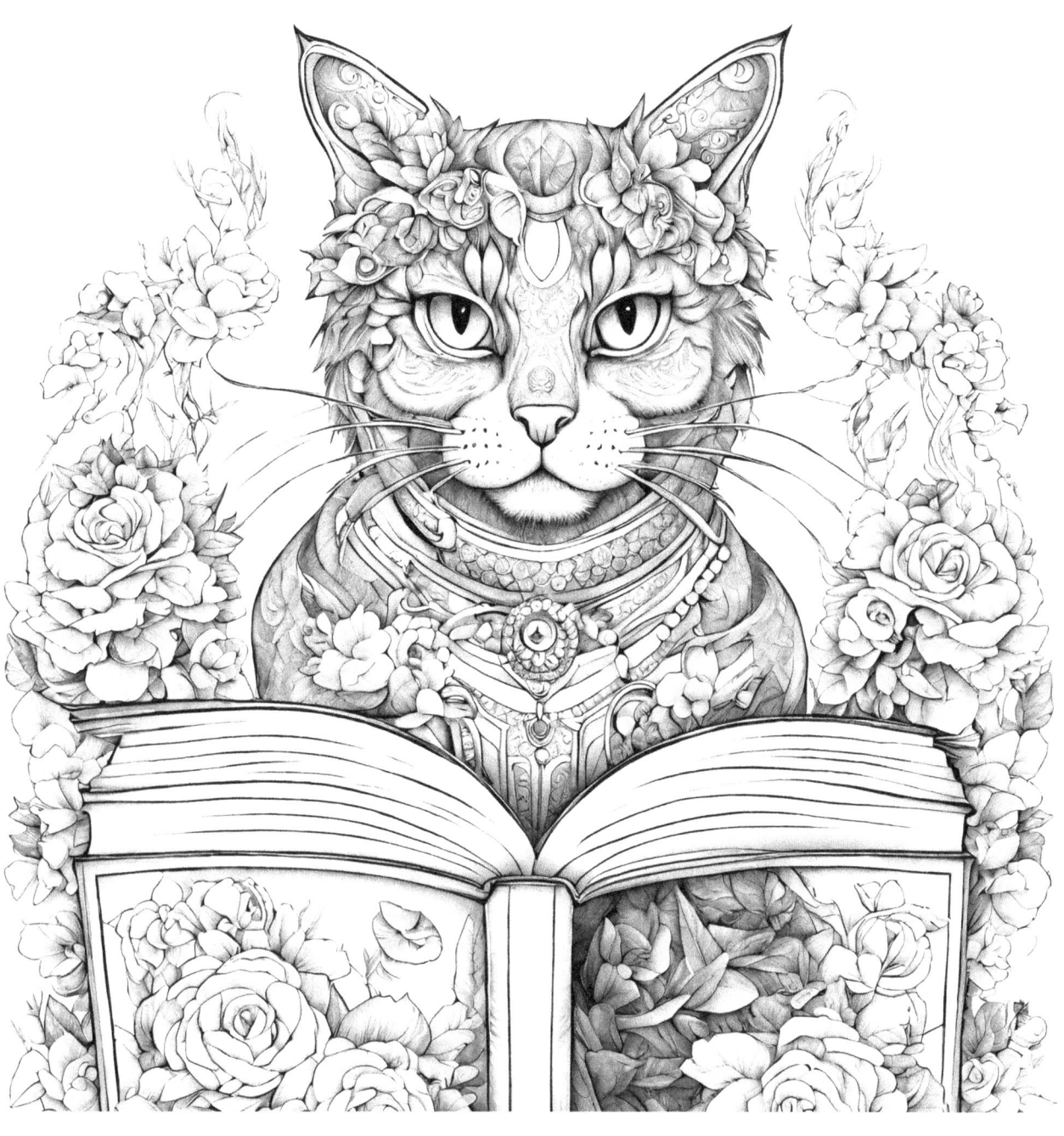

**IN ANCIENT TIMES CATS WERE WORSHIPPED AS GODS,
THEY HAVE NOT FORGOTTEN THIS**

TERRY PRATCHETT

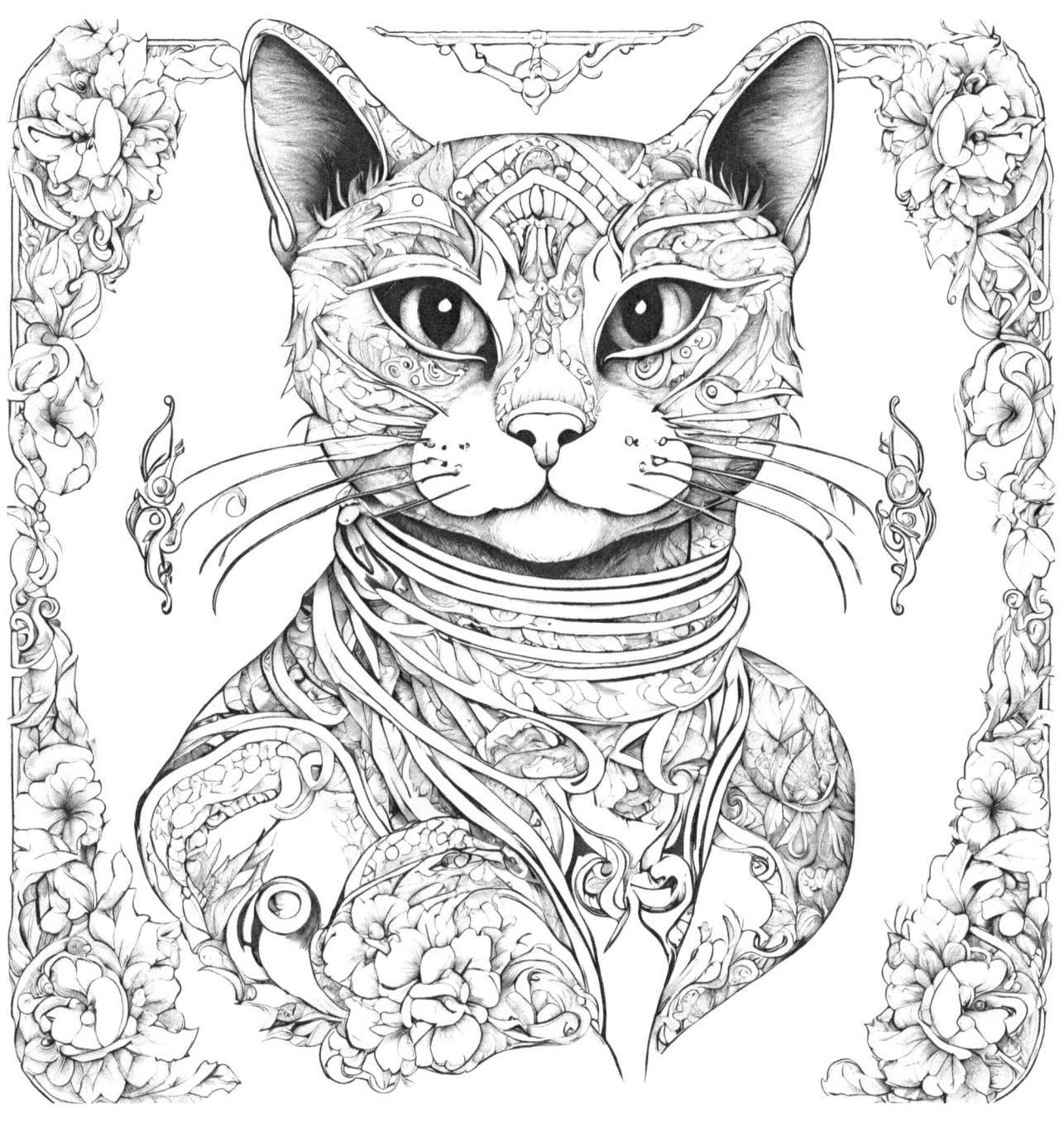

I HAD BEEN TOLD THAT THE TRAINING PROCEDURE WITH CATS WAS DIFFICULT. IT´S NOT. MINE HAD ME TRAINED IN TWO DAYS.

BILL DANA

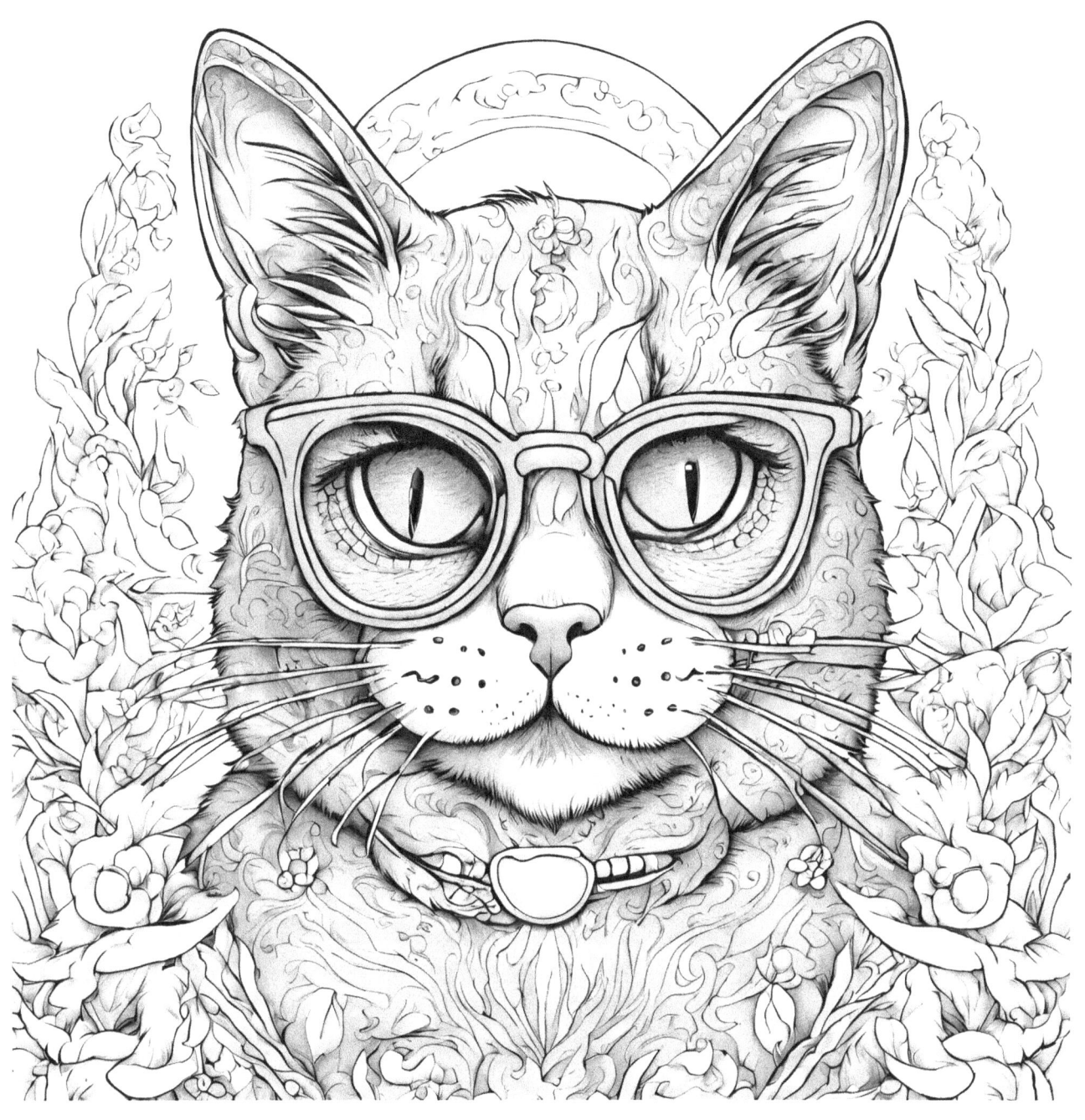

A CAT HAS ABSOLUTE EMOTIONAL HONESTY: HUMAN BEINGS, FOR ONE REASON OR ANOTHER, MAY HIDE THEIR FEELINGS, BUT A CAT DOES NOT

ERNEST HEMINGWAY

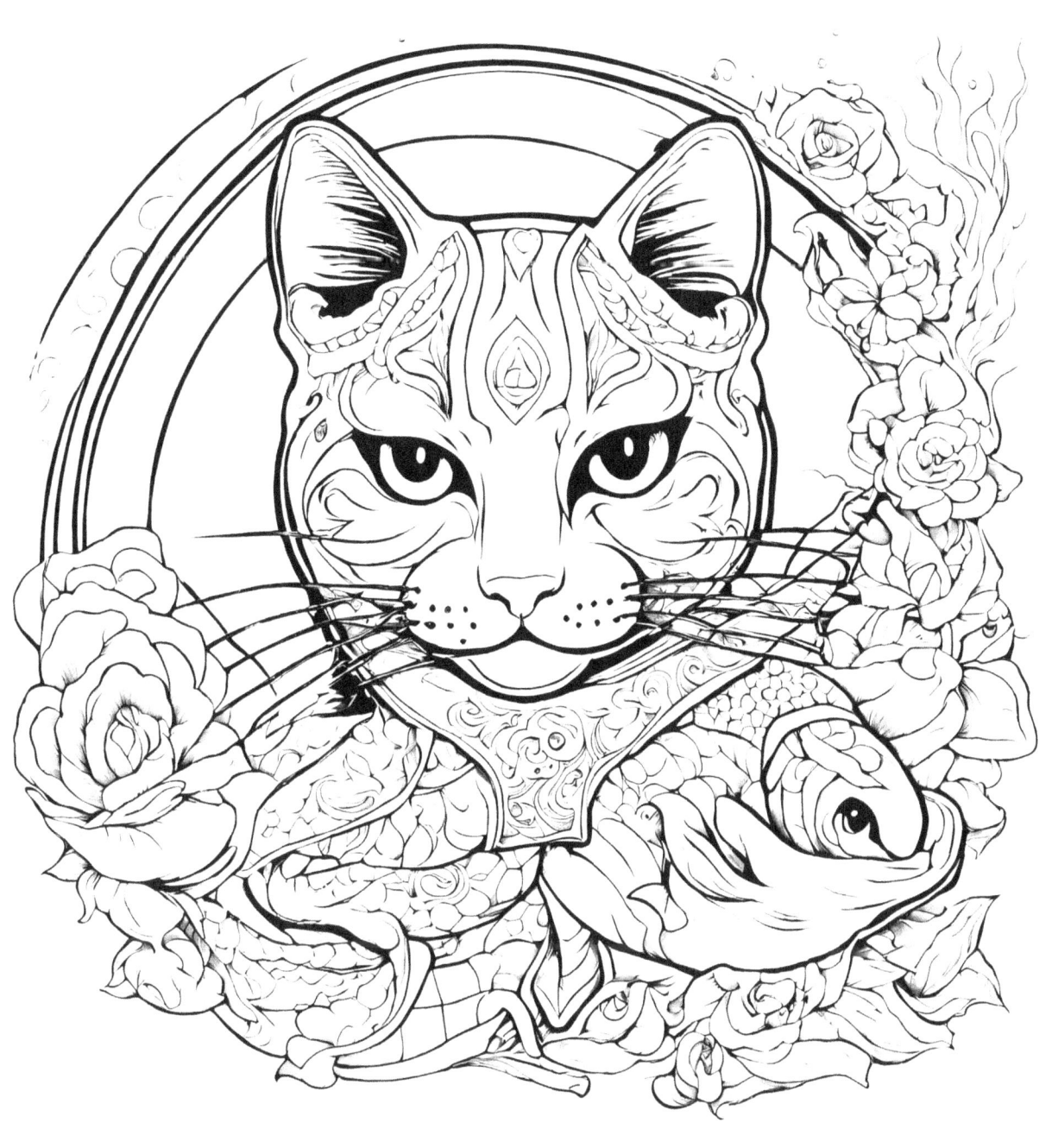

CATS ARE INQUISITIVE, BUT HATE TO ADMIT IT

MASON COOLEY

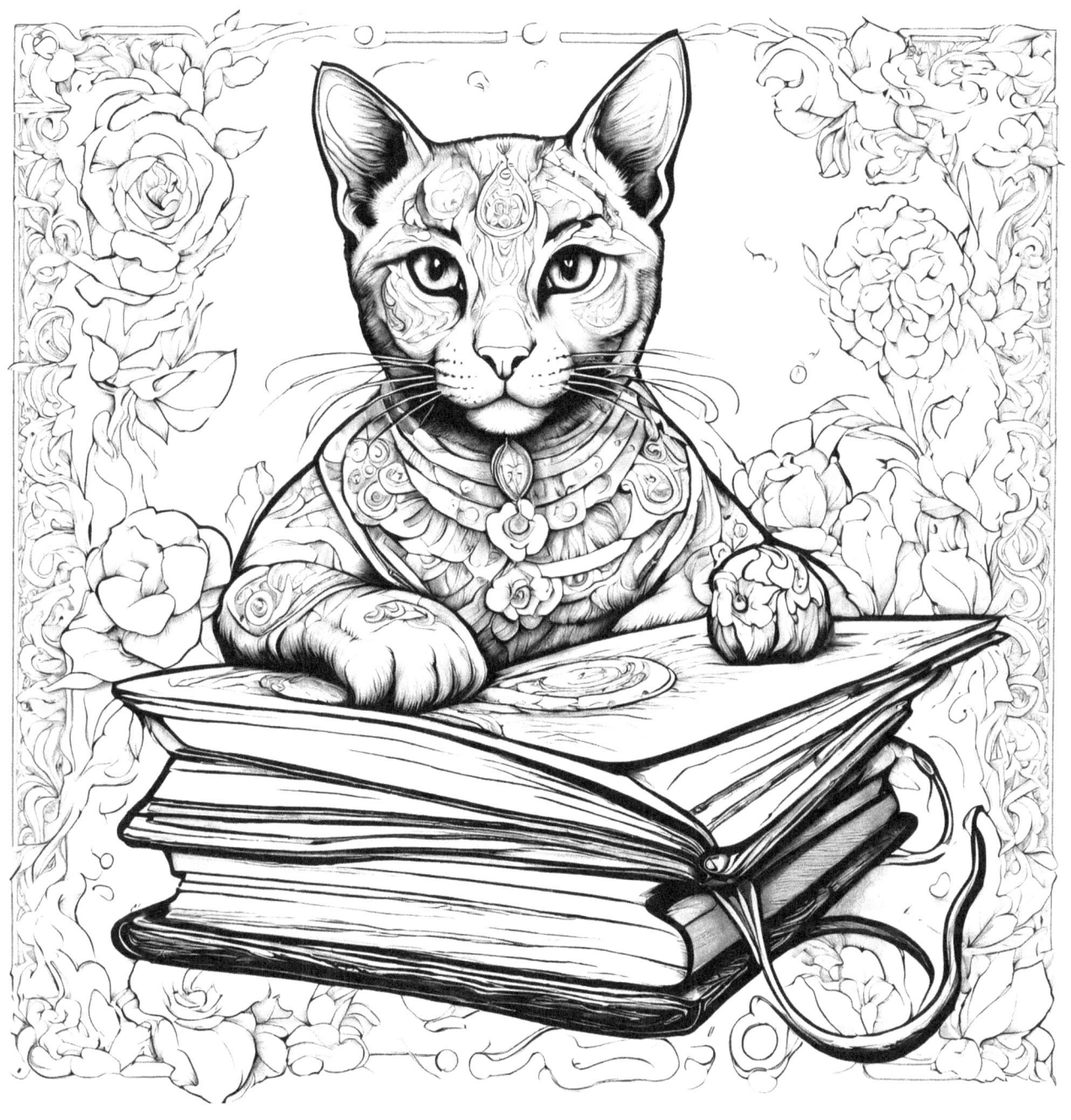

AS ANYONE WHO HAS EVER BEEN AROUND A CAT FOR
ANY LENGTH OF TIME WELL KNOWS, CATS HAVE
ENORMOUS PATIENCE WITH THE LIMITATIONS OF THE
HUMANKIND

CLEVELAND AMORY

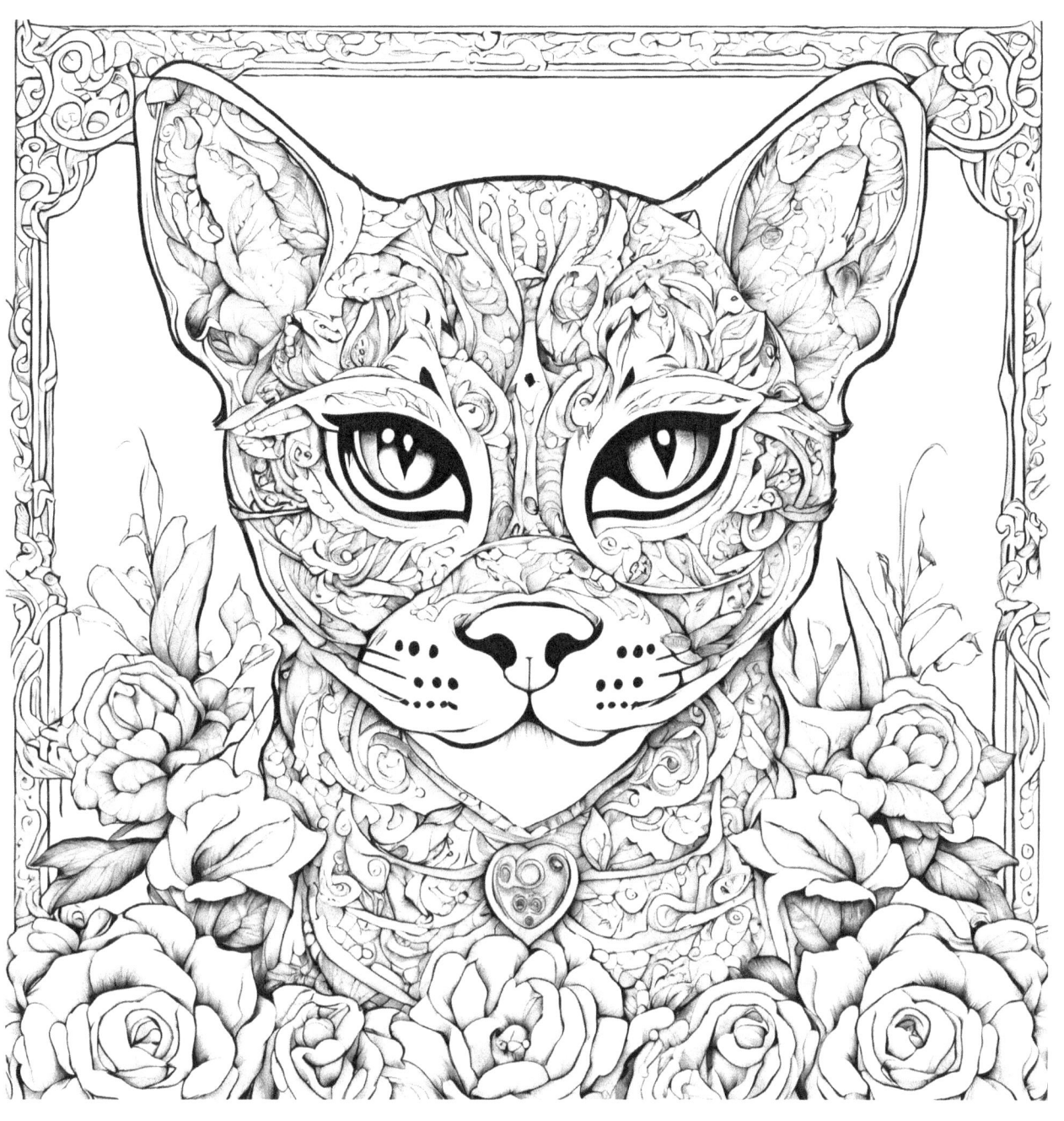

CATS CHOOSE US; WE DON'T OWN THEM.

KRISTIN CAST

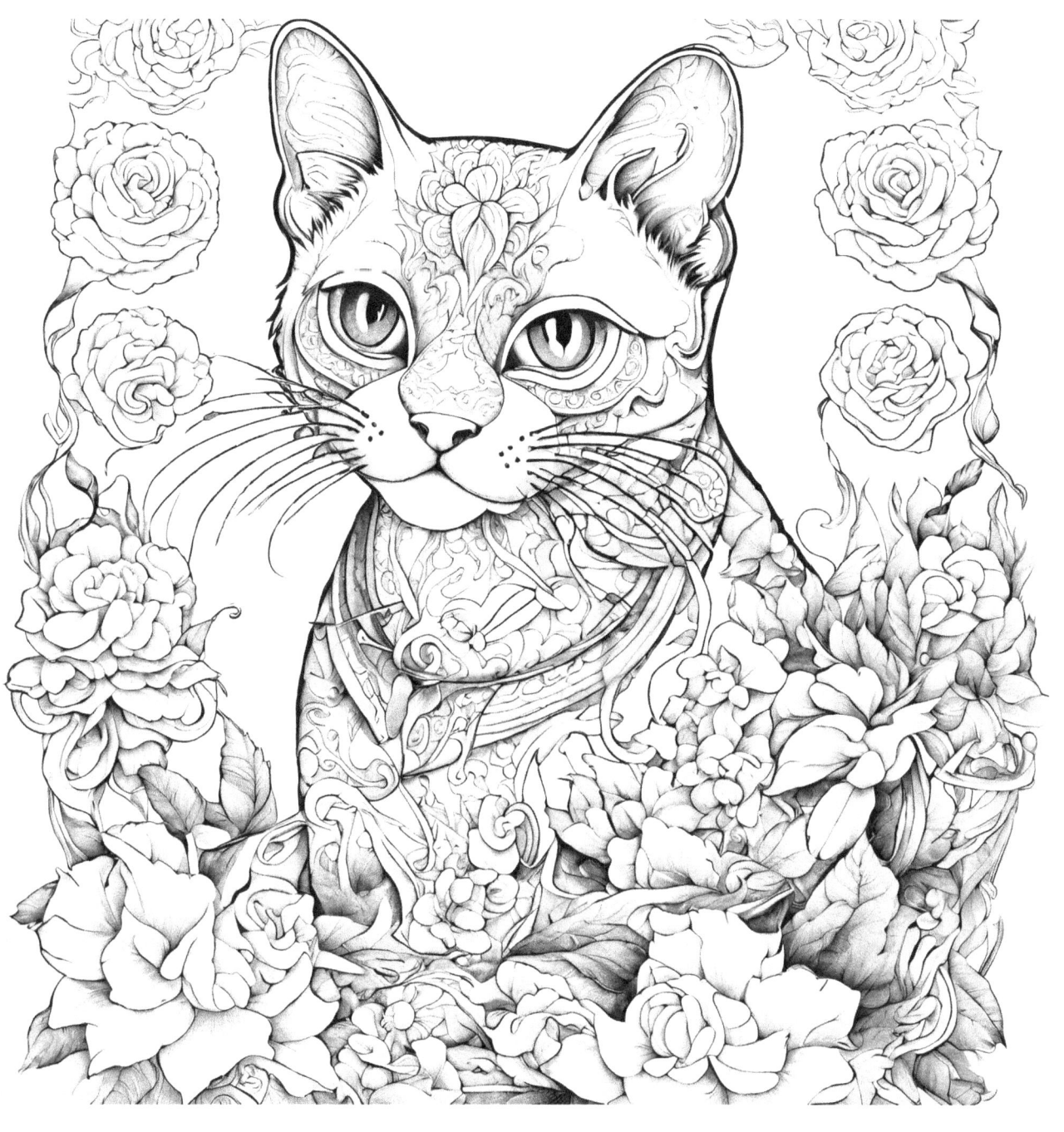

**I HAVE STUDIED MANY PHILOSOPHERS AND MANY CATS.
THE WISDOM OF CATS IS INFINITELY SUPERIOR.**

HIPPOLYTE TAINE

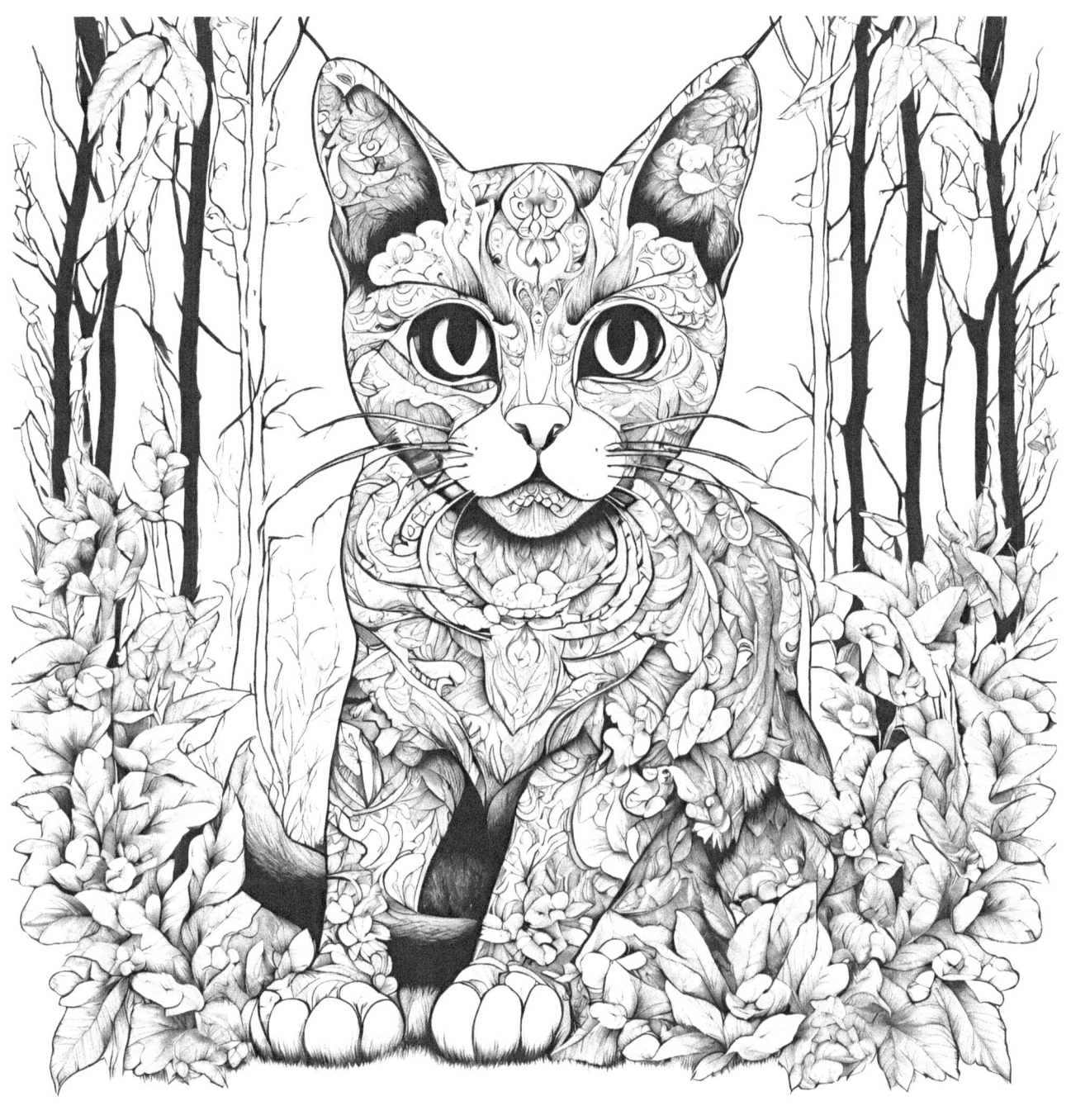

CATS ARE THE EPITOME OF MISCHIEF WITH A TOUCH OF CHARM.

UNKNOWN

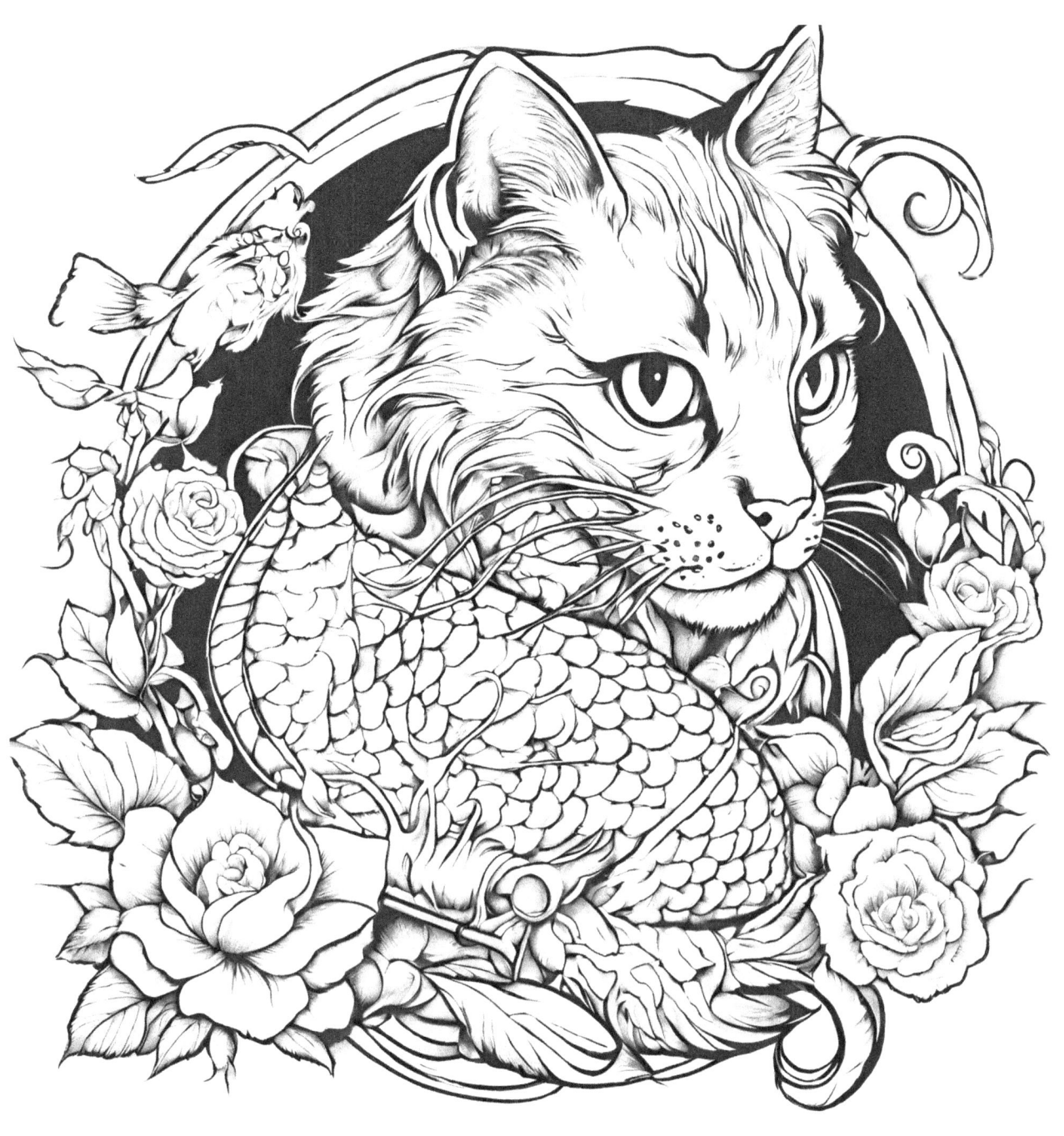

CATS ARE CONNOISSEURS OF COMFORT

JAMES HERRIOT

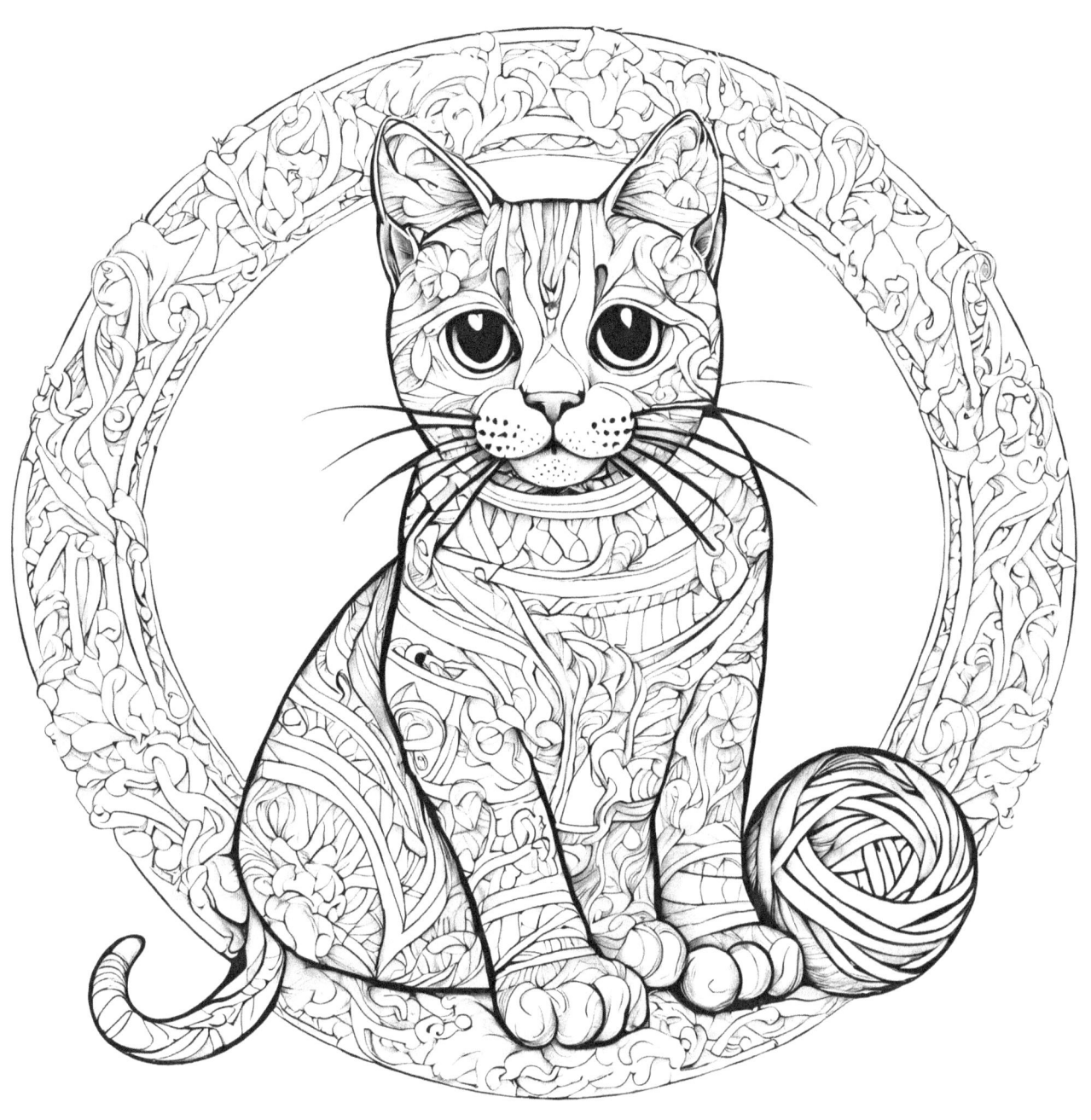

CATS ARE INTENDED TO TEACH US THAT NOT EVERYTHING IN NATURE HAS A PURPOSE.

GARRISON KEILLOR

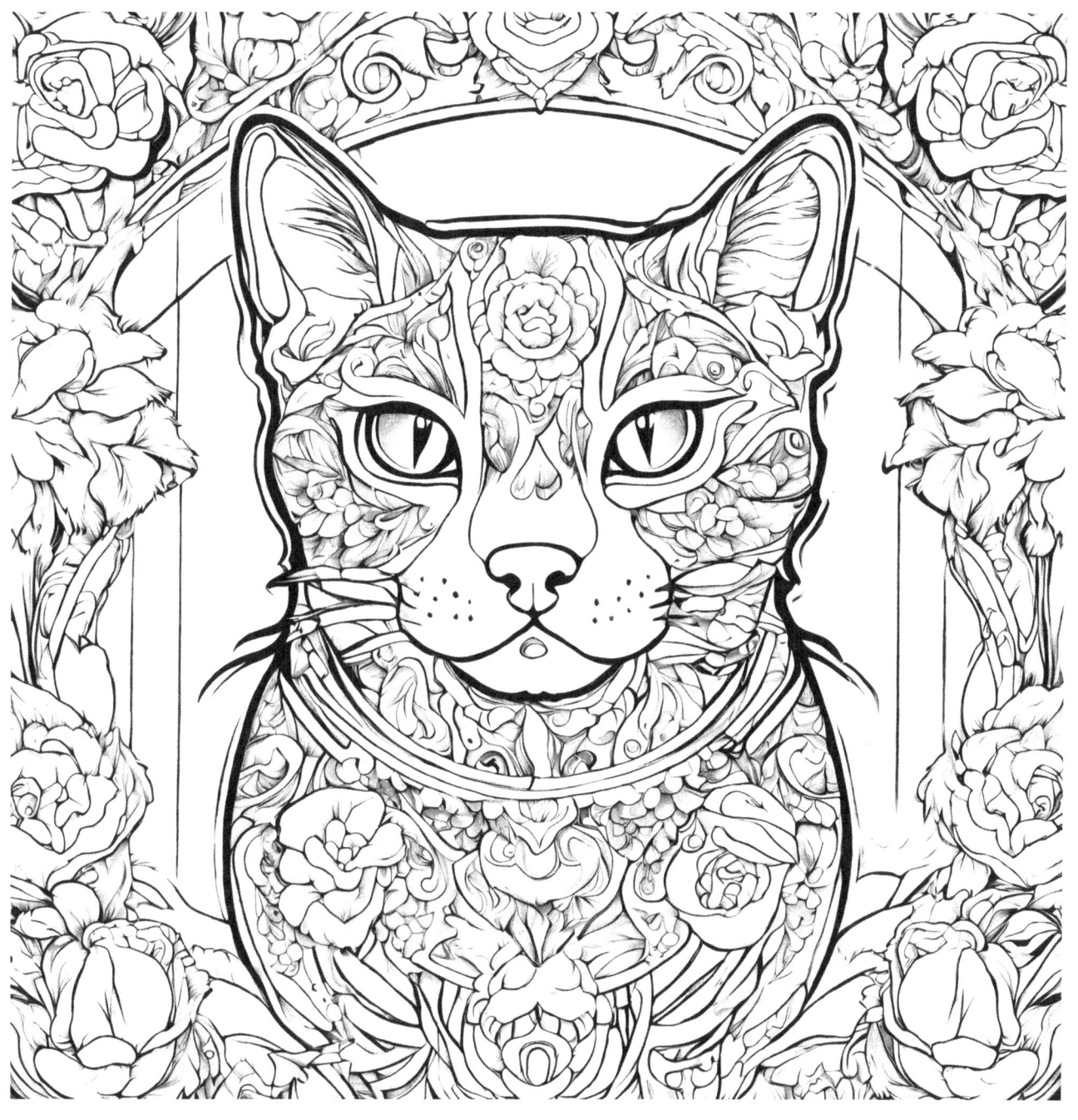

I´M NOT SURE WHY I LIKE CATS SO MUCH. I MEAN, THEY
´RE REALLY CUTE OBVIOUSLY.THEY ARE BOTH WILD AND
DOMESTIC AT THE SAME TIME

MICHAEL SHOWALTER

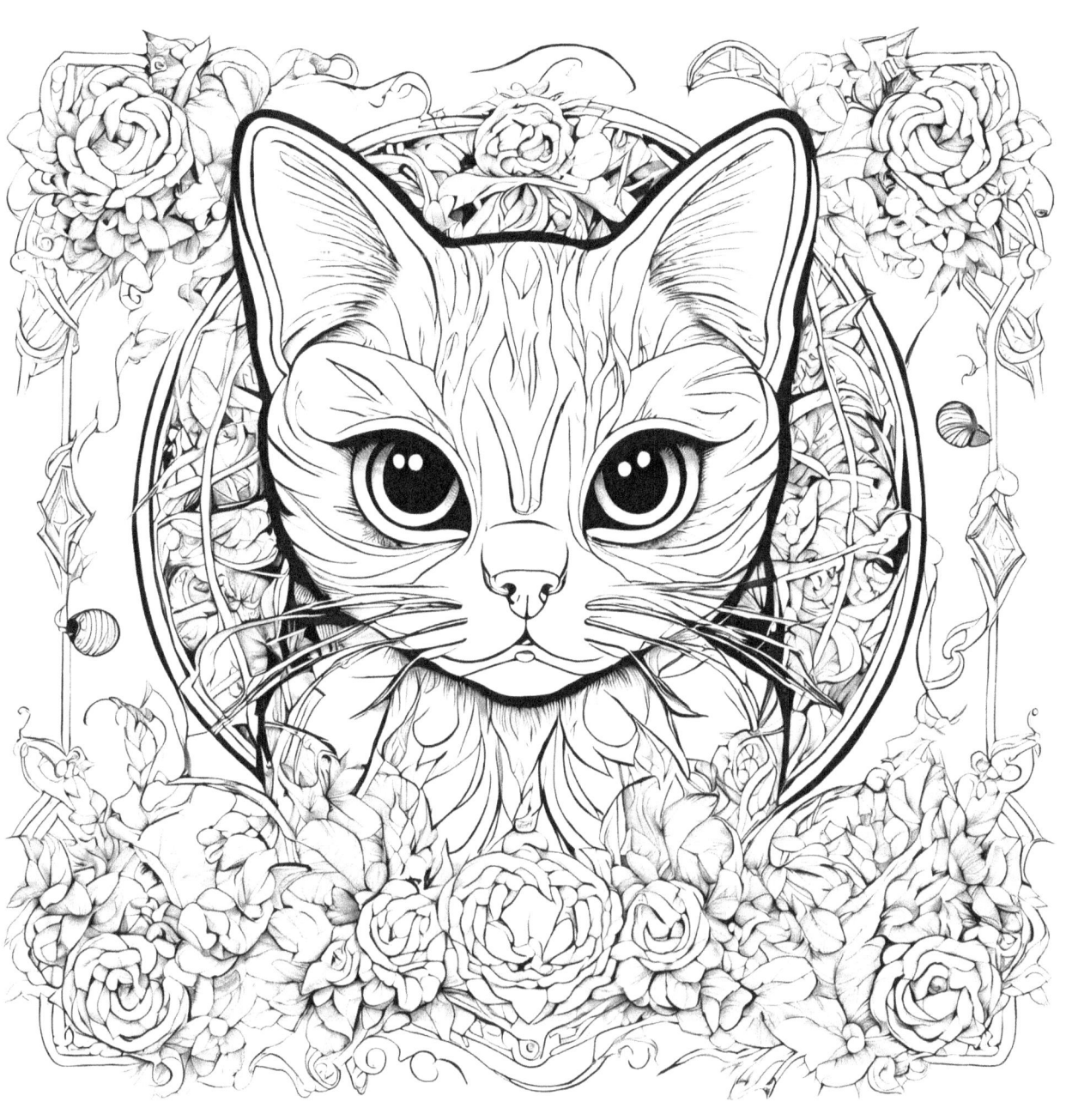

CATS CAN WORK OUT MATHEMATICALLY THE EXACT PLACE TO SIT THAT WILL CAUSE MOST INCONVENIENCE.

PAM BROWN

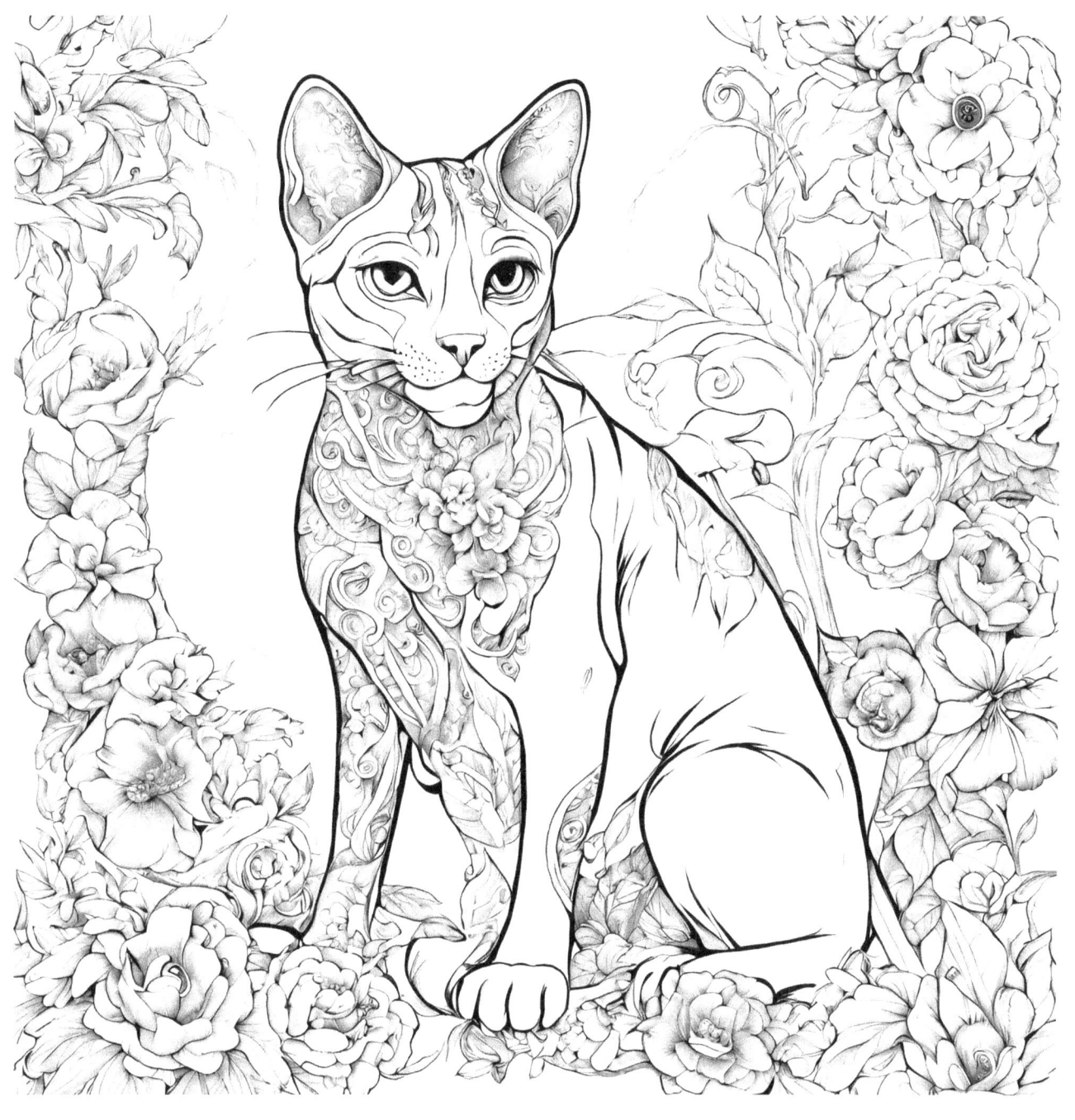

TO CAT OR NOT TO CAT, THAT IS NOT THE QUESTION!

MAYTE LÓPEZ LÓPEZ

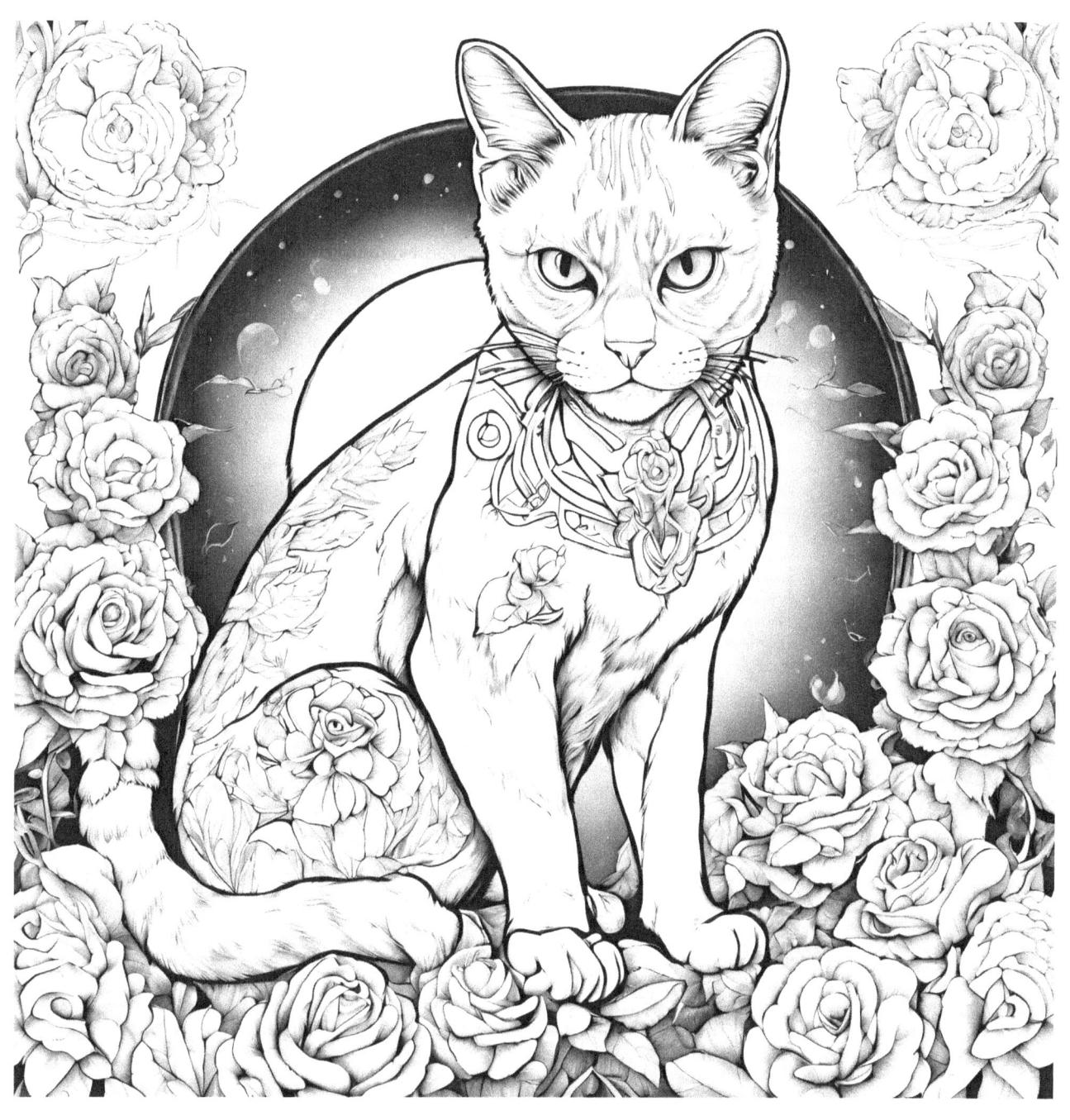

YOU CAN LOOK AT A SLEEPING CAT AND FEEL TENSE

JANE PAULEY

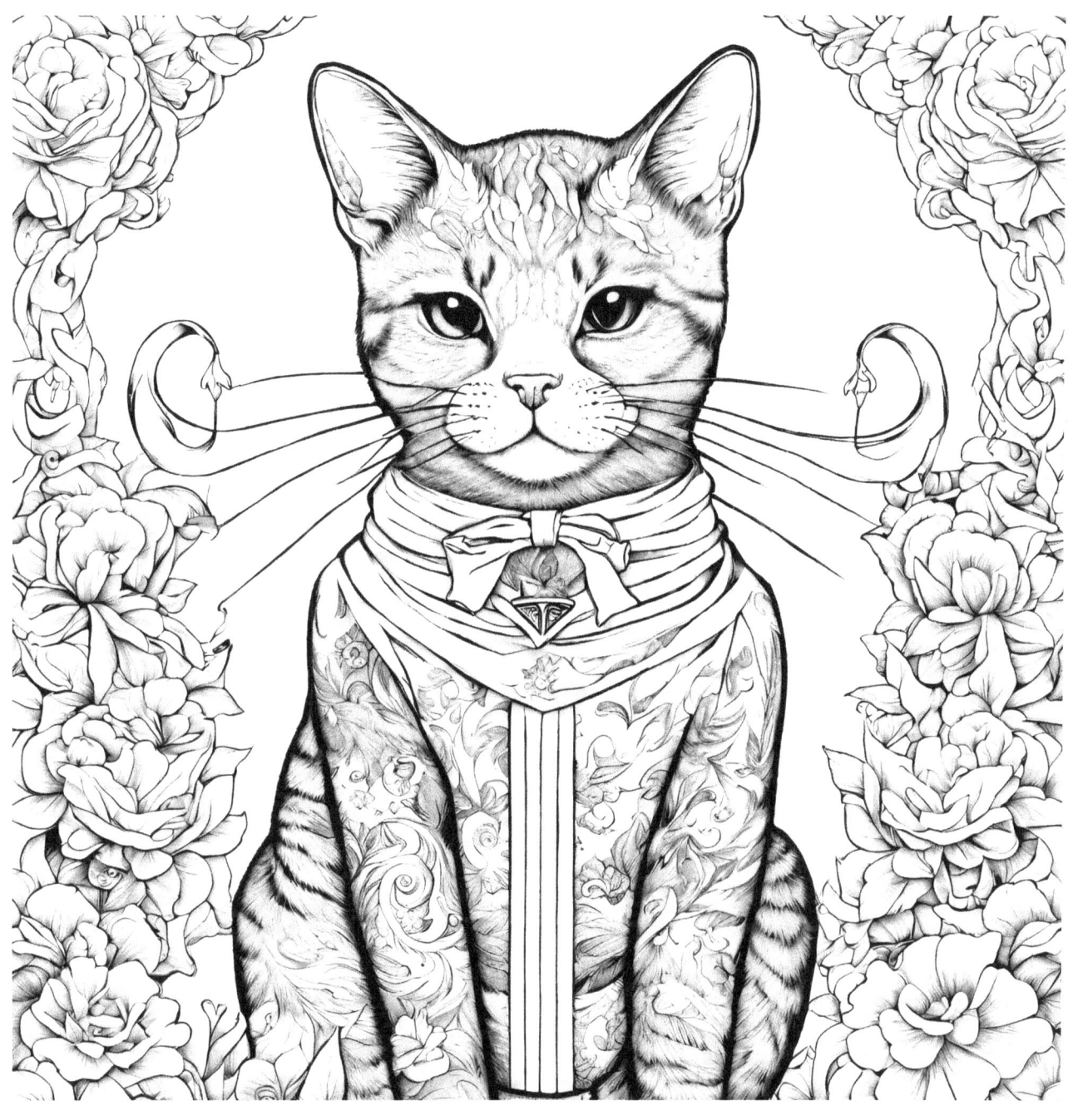

CATS SEEM TO GO ON THE PRINCIPLE THAT IT NEVER DOES ANY HARM TO ASK FOR WHAT YOU WANT.

JOSEPH WOOD KRUTCH

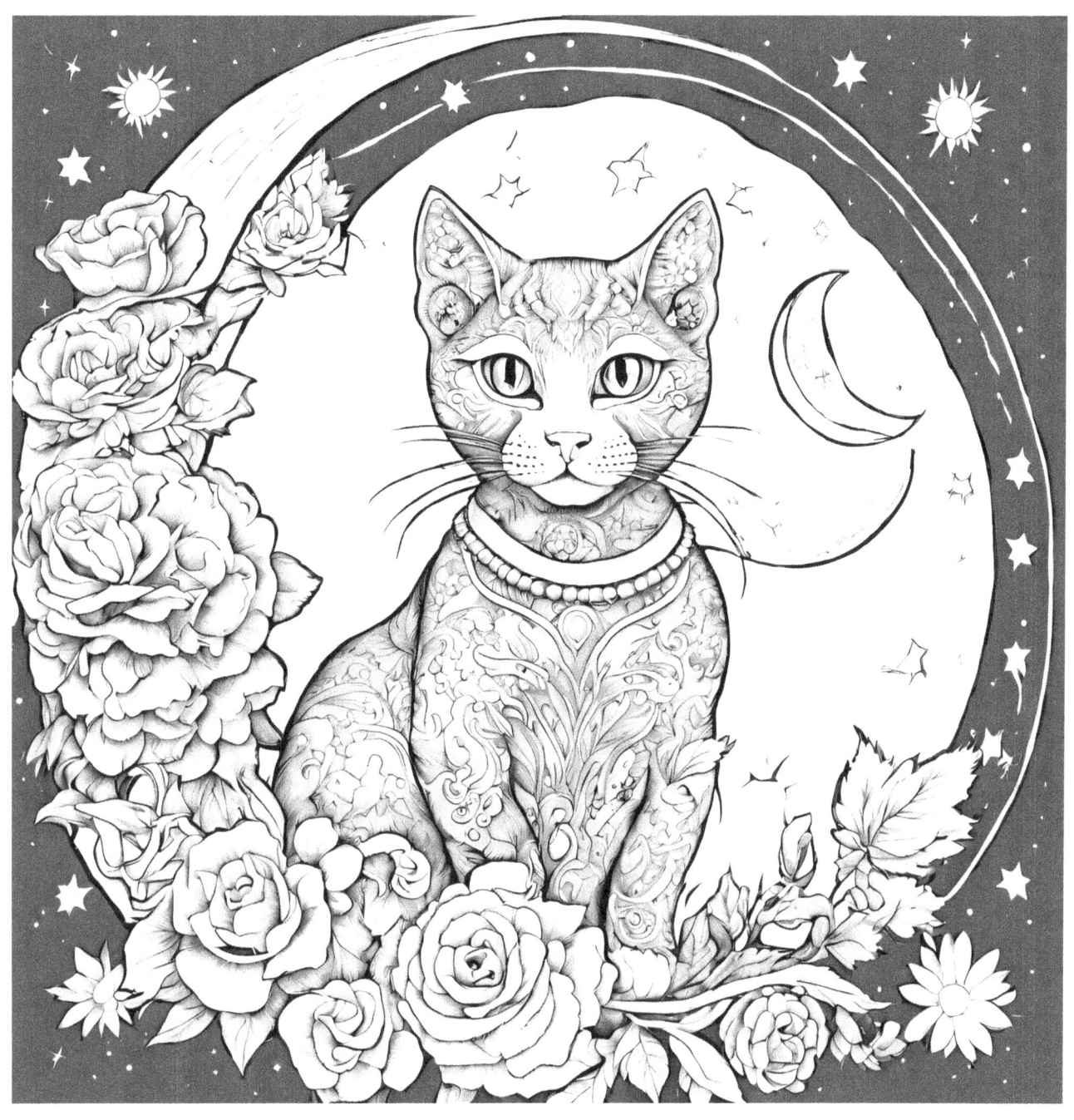

ONE CAT JUST LEADS TO ANOTHER

ERNEST HEMINGWAY

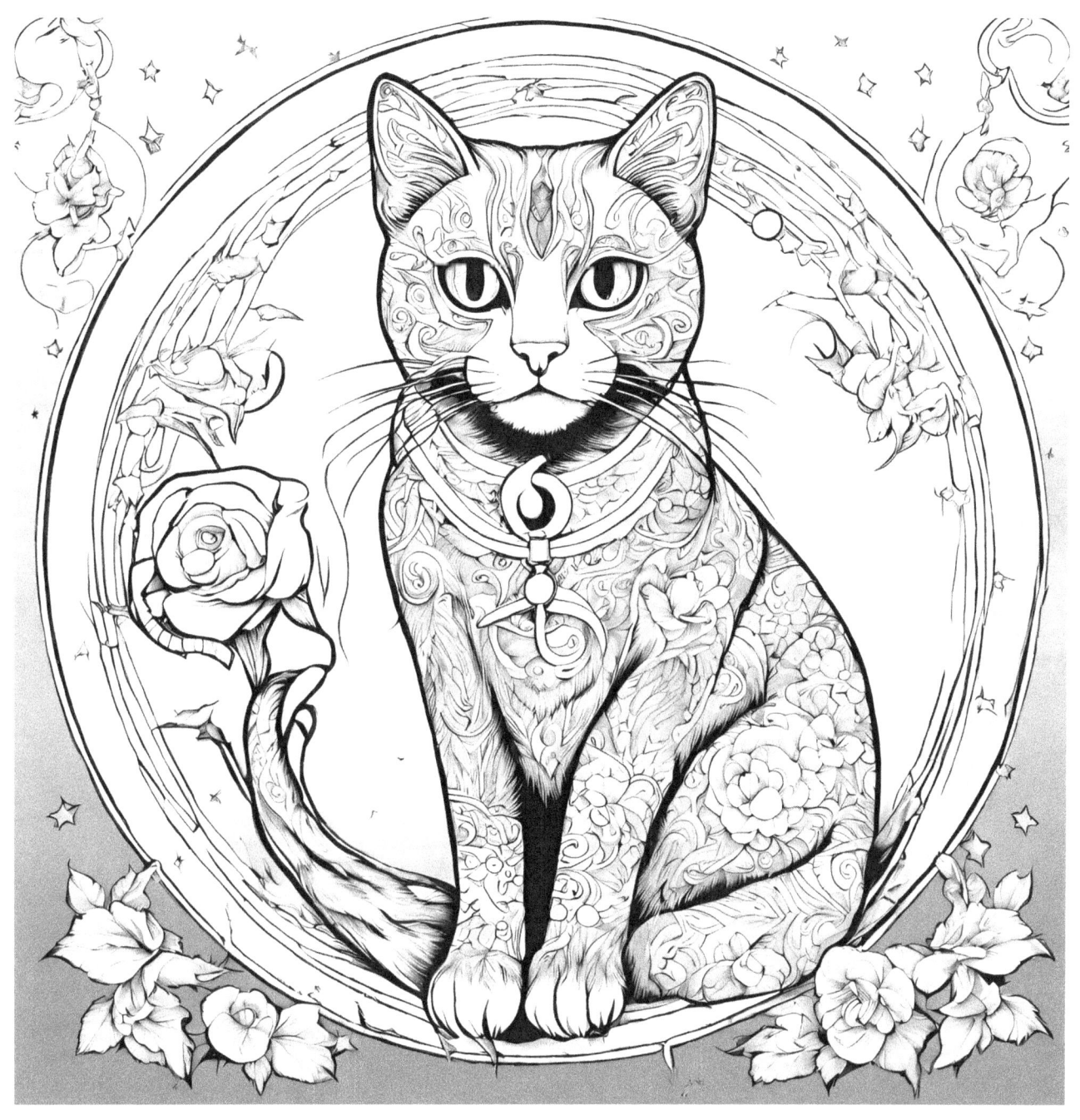

A HAPPY ARRANGEMENT: MANY PEOPLE PREFER CATS TO OTHER PEOPLE, AND MANY CATS PREFER PEOPLE TO OTHER CATS.

MASON COOLEY

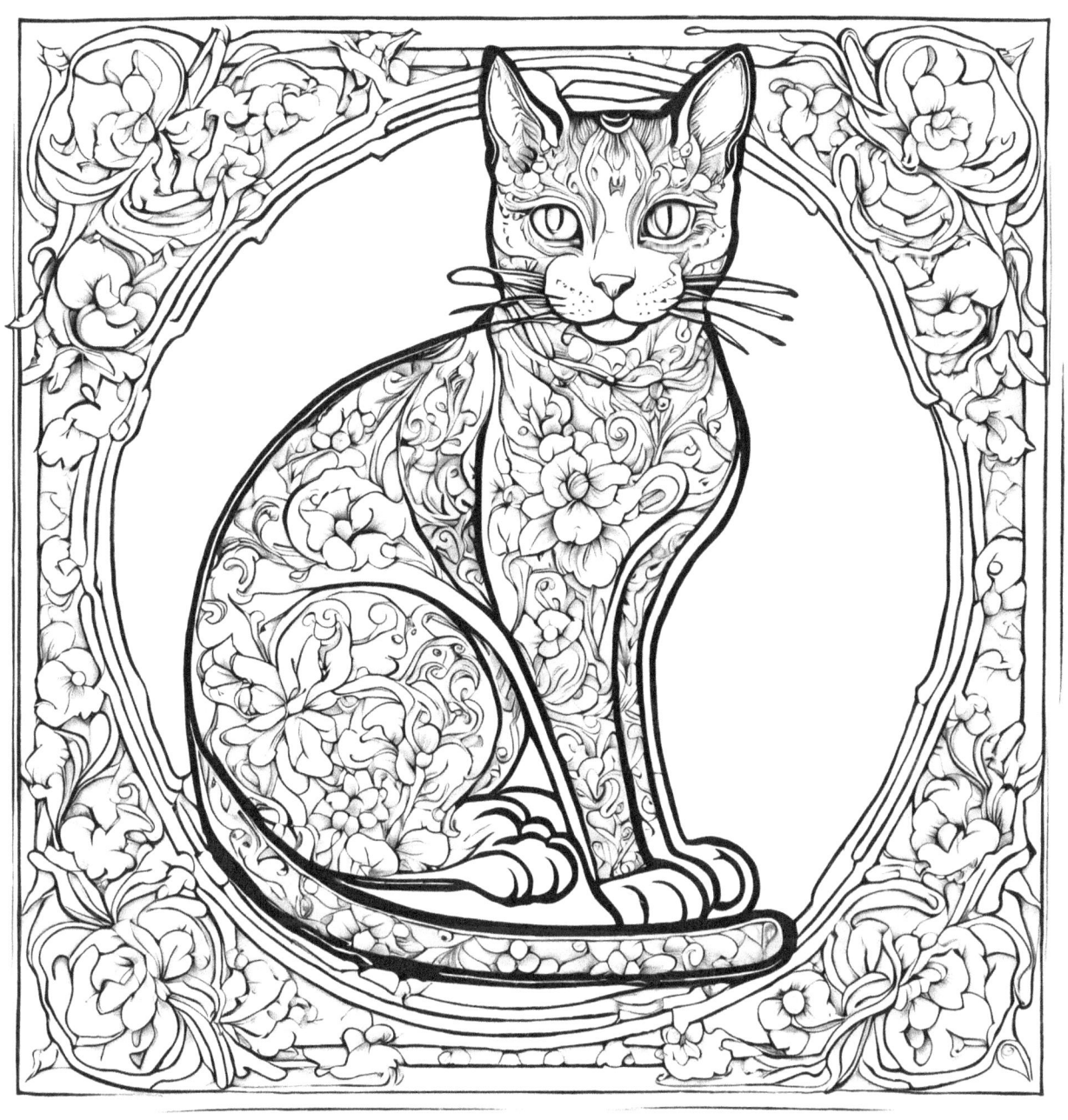

A CAT IS A PUZZLE FOR WHICH THERE IS NO SOLUTION.

HAZEL NICHOLSON

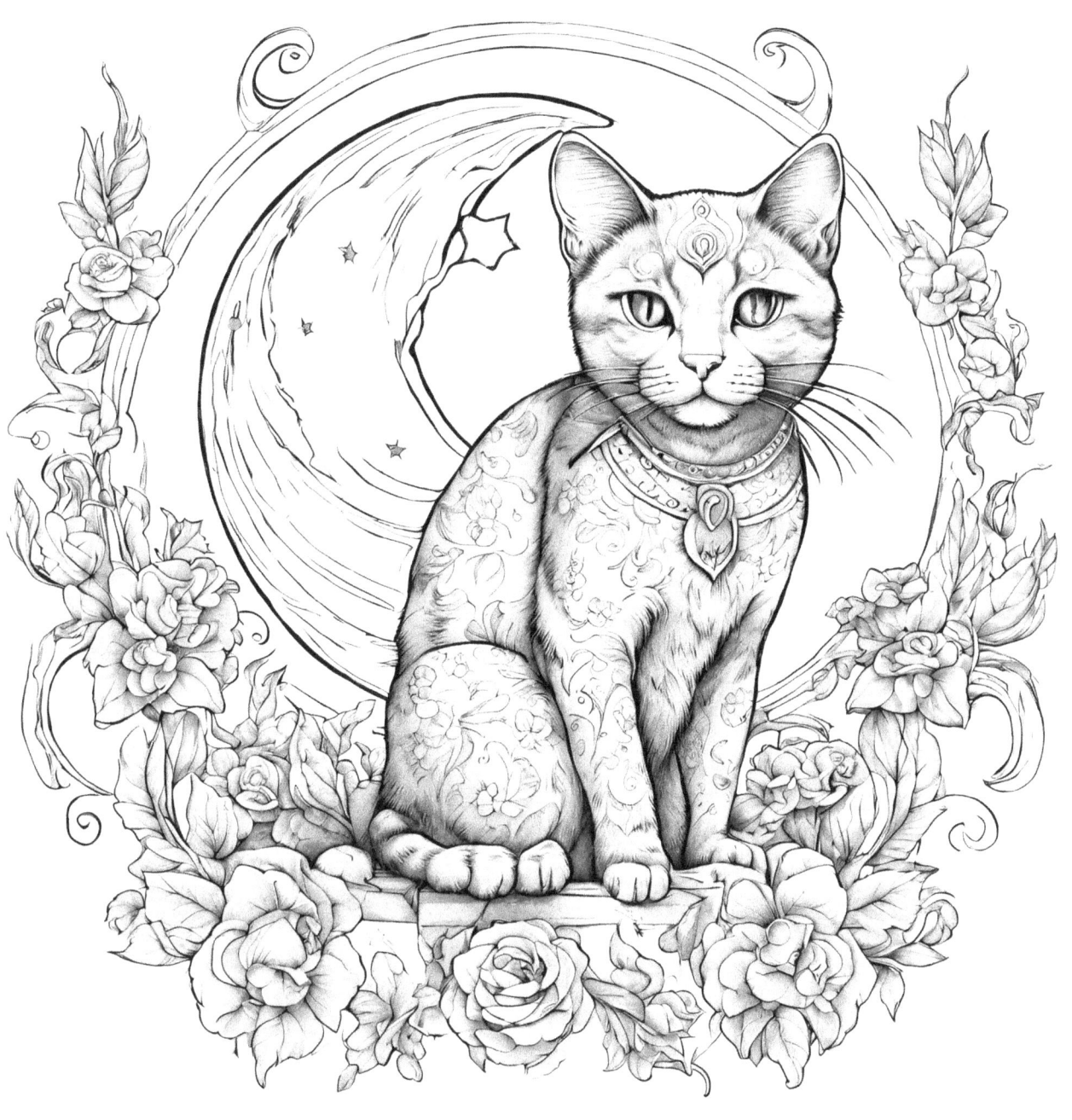

CATS WILL OUTSMART DOGS EVERY TIME

JOHN GROGAN

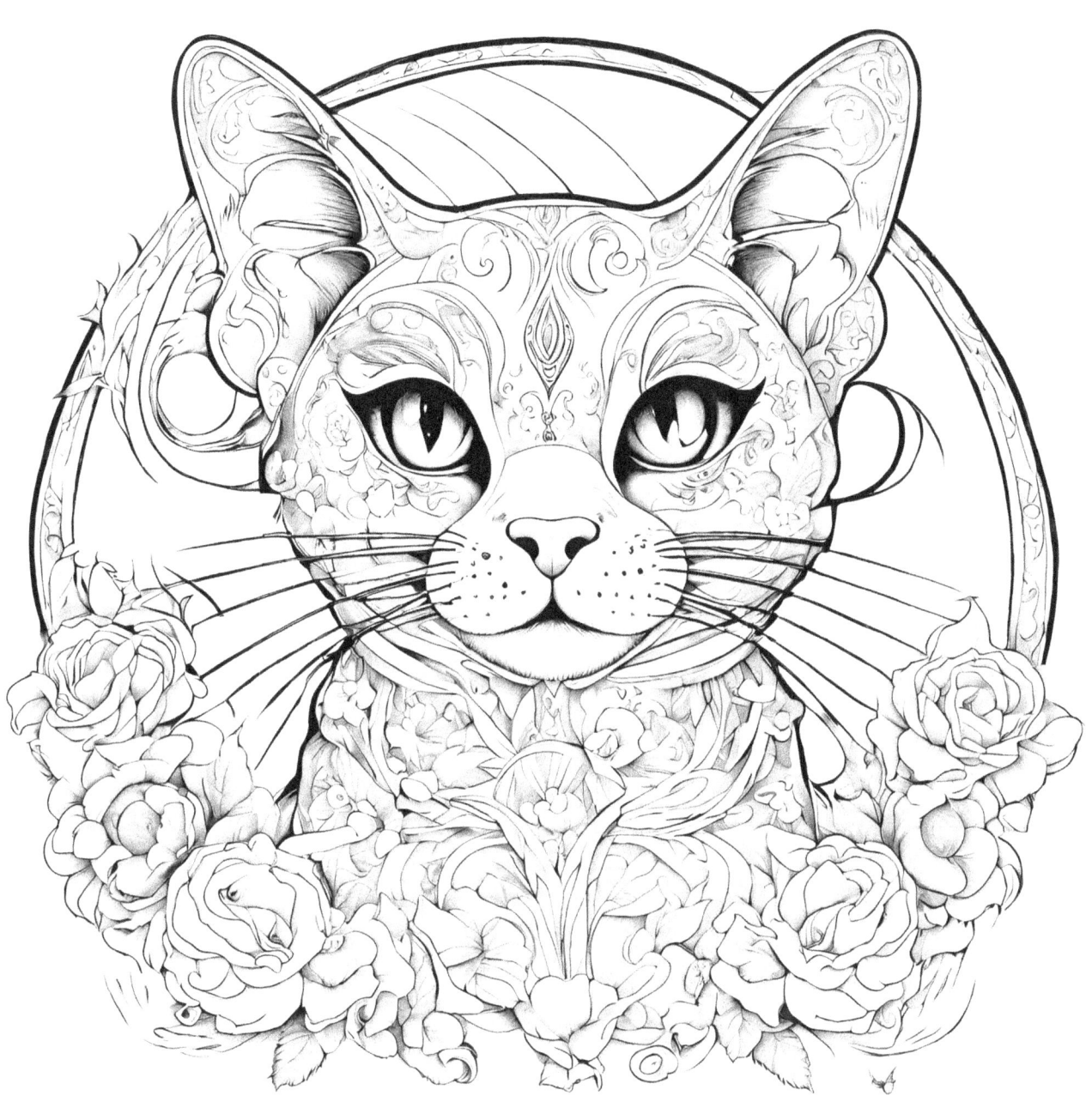

**NO MATTER HOW MUCH CATS FIGHT, THERE ALWAYS
SEEM TO BE PLENTY OF KITTENS**

ABRAHAM LINCOLN

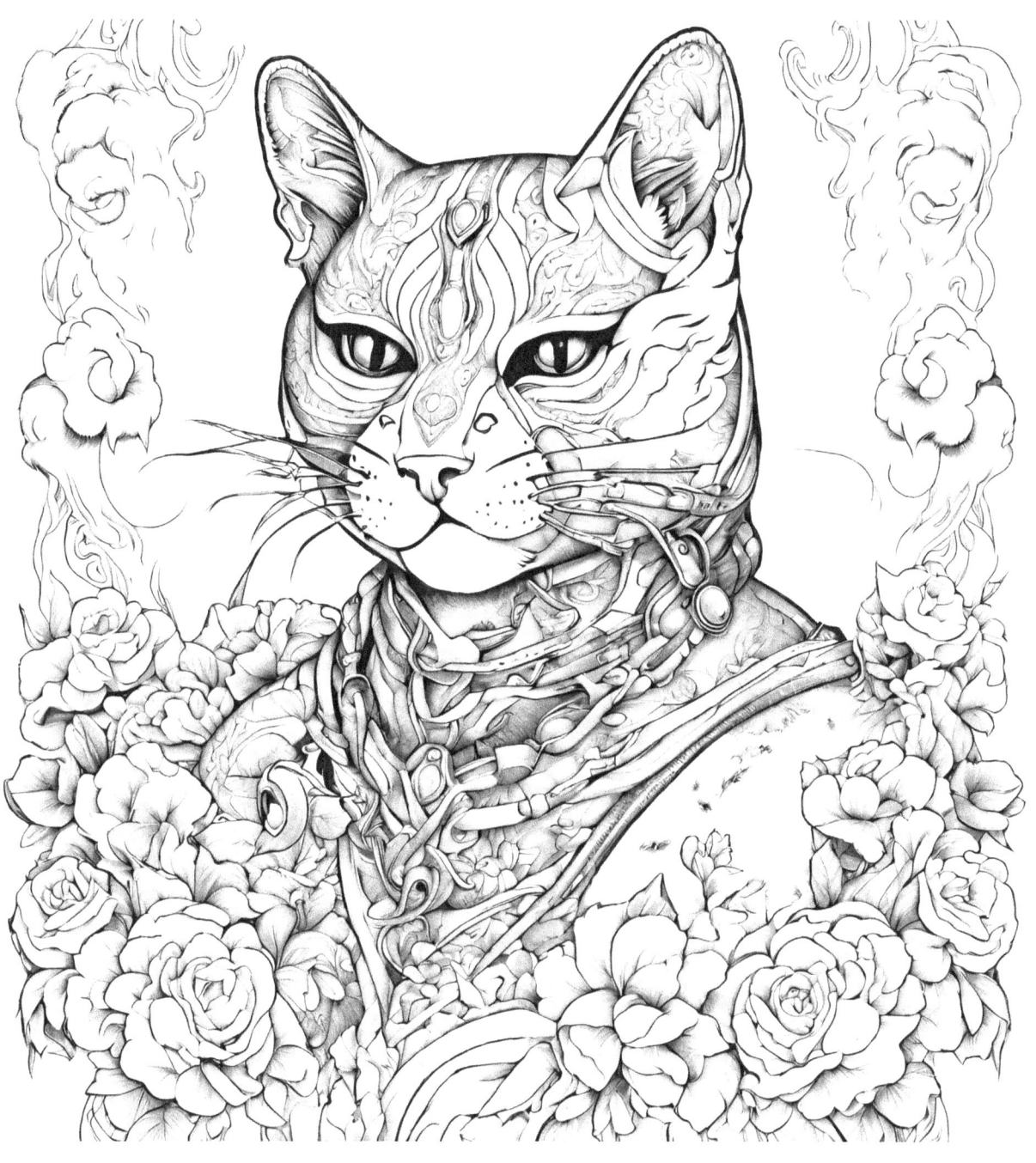

CATS ARE A MYSTERIOUS KIND OF FOLK.

WALTER SCOTT

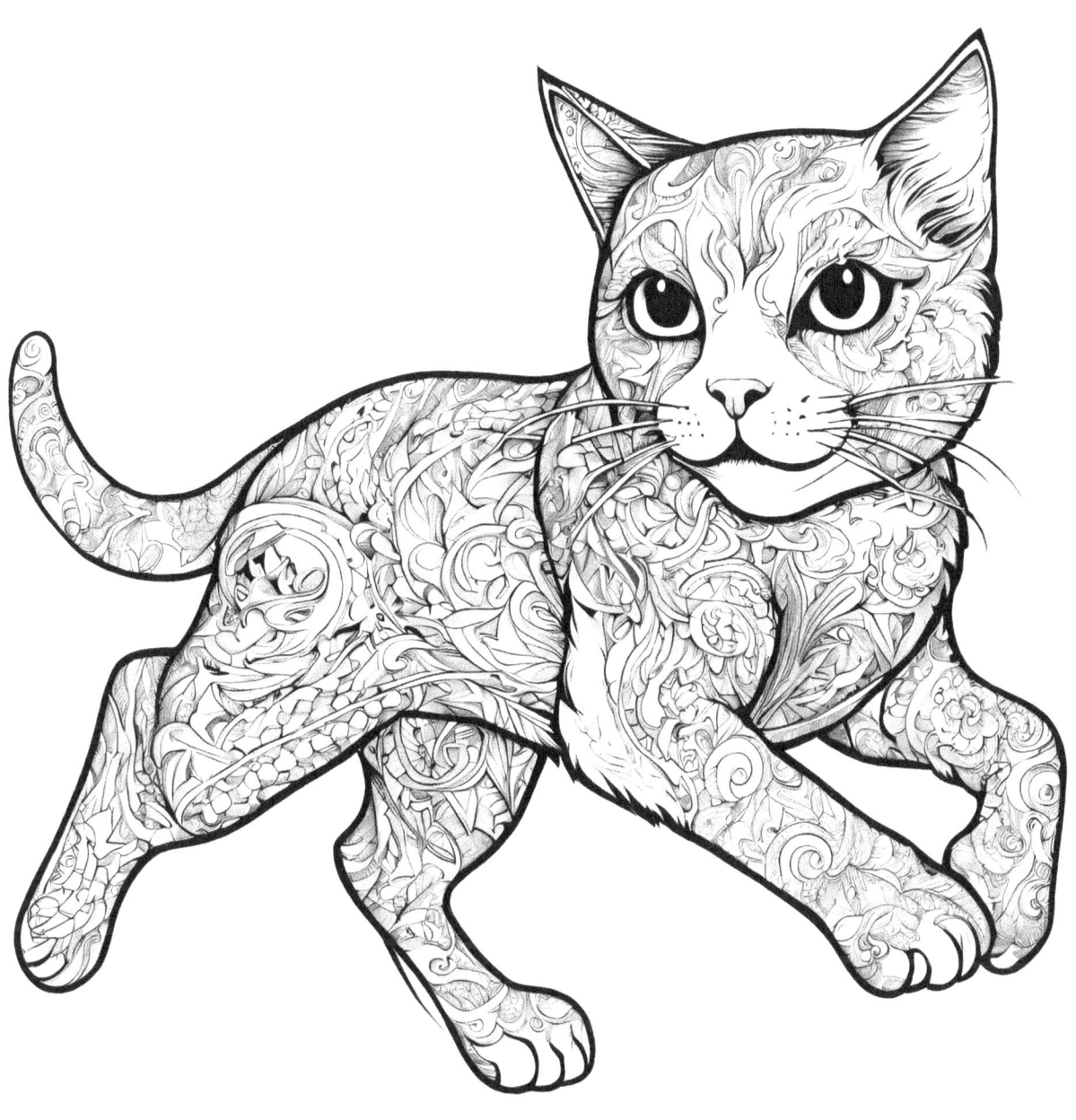

THE SMALLEST FELINE IS A MASTERPIECE

LEONARDO DA VINCI

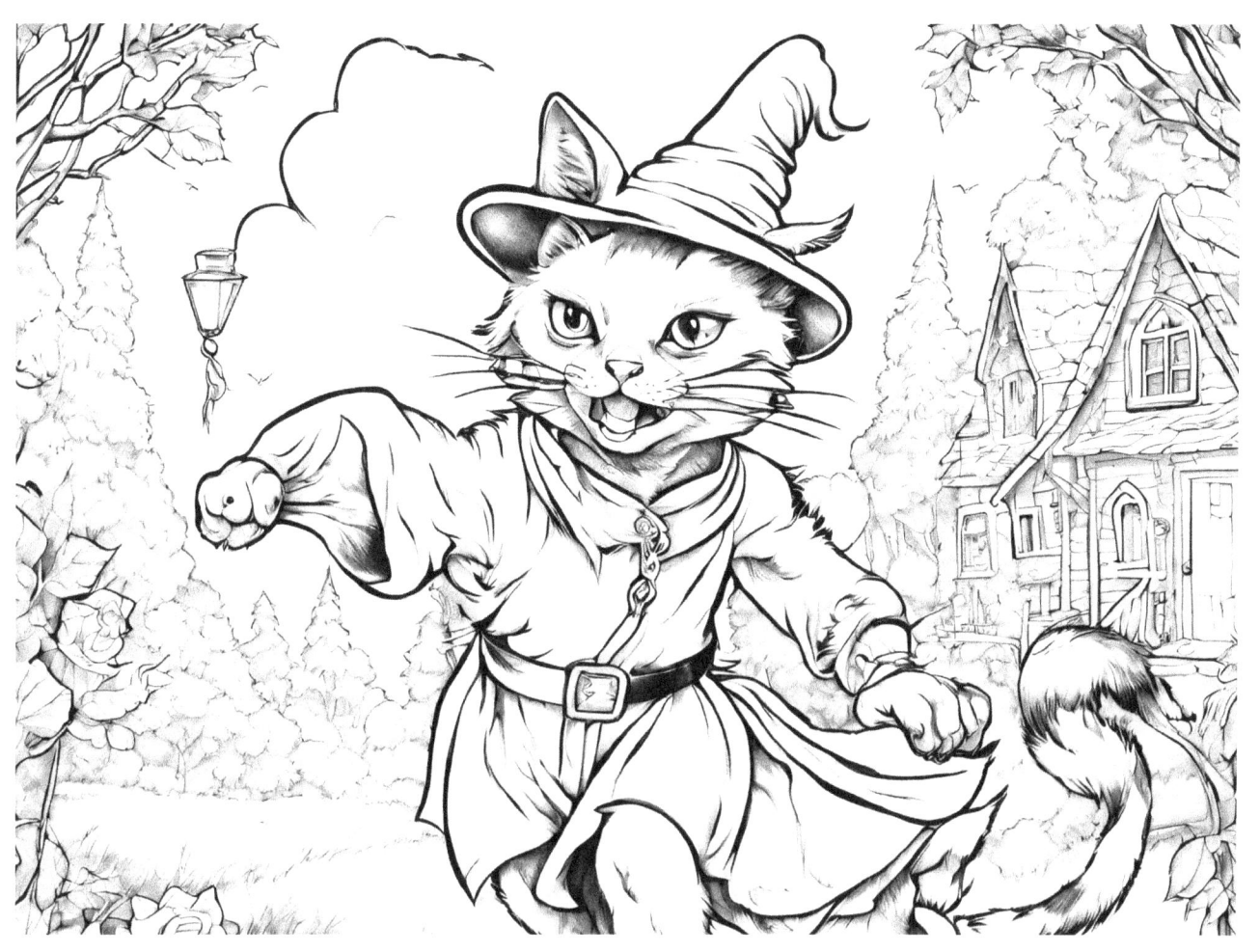

**THERE ARE TWO MEANS OF REFUGE
FROM THE MISERIES OF LIFE:
MUSIC AND CATS.**

ALBERT SCHWEITZER

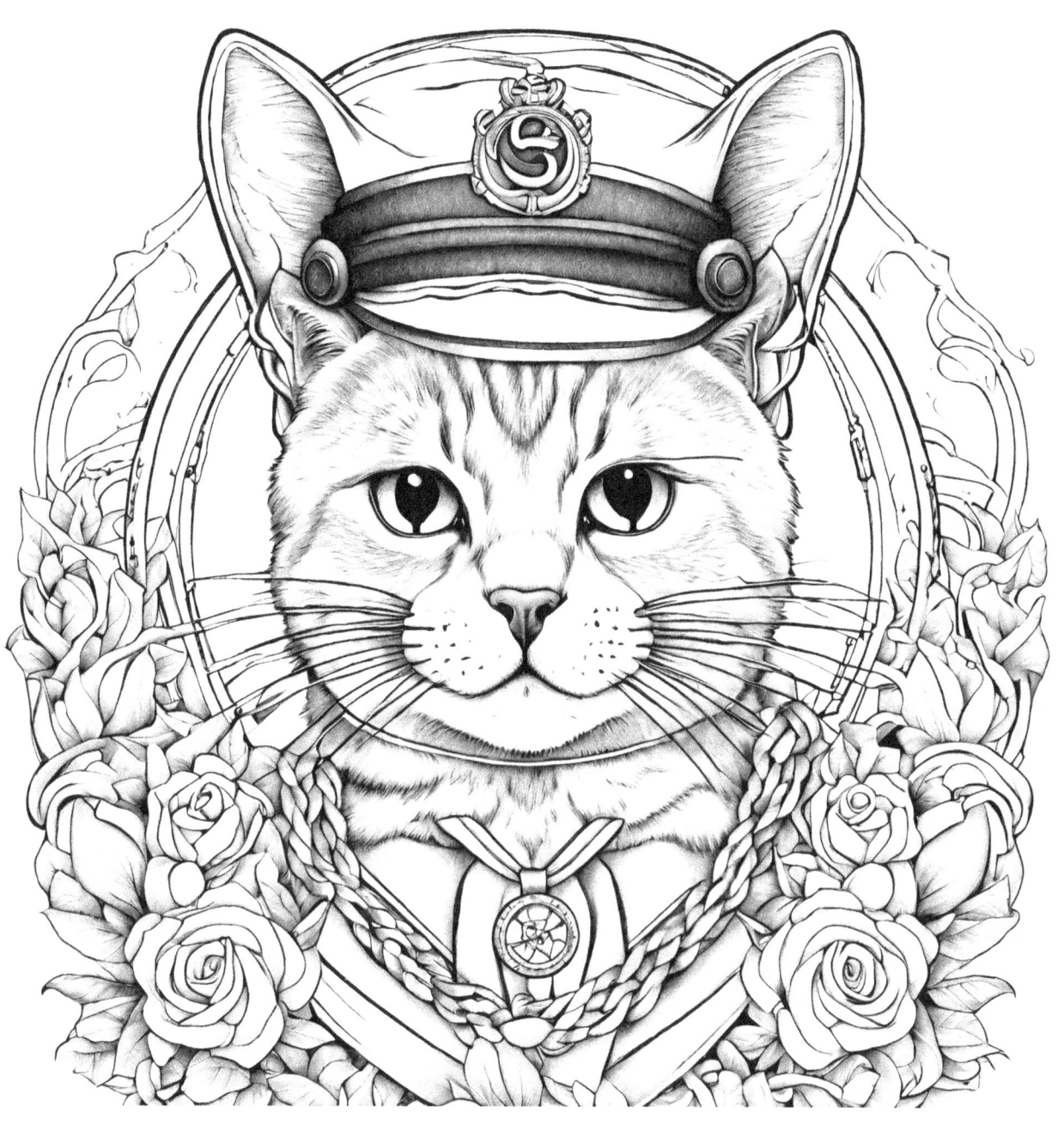

CATS HAVE IT ALL: ADMIRATION, ENDLESS NAPS, AND COMPANY ONLY WHEN THEY WANT IT.

ROD MCKUEN

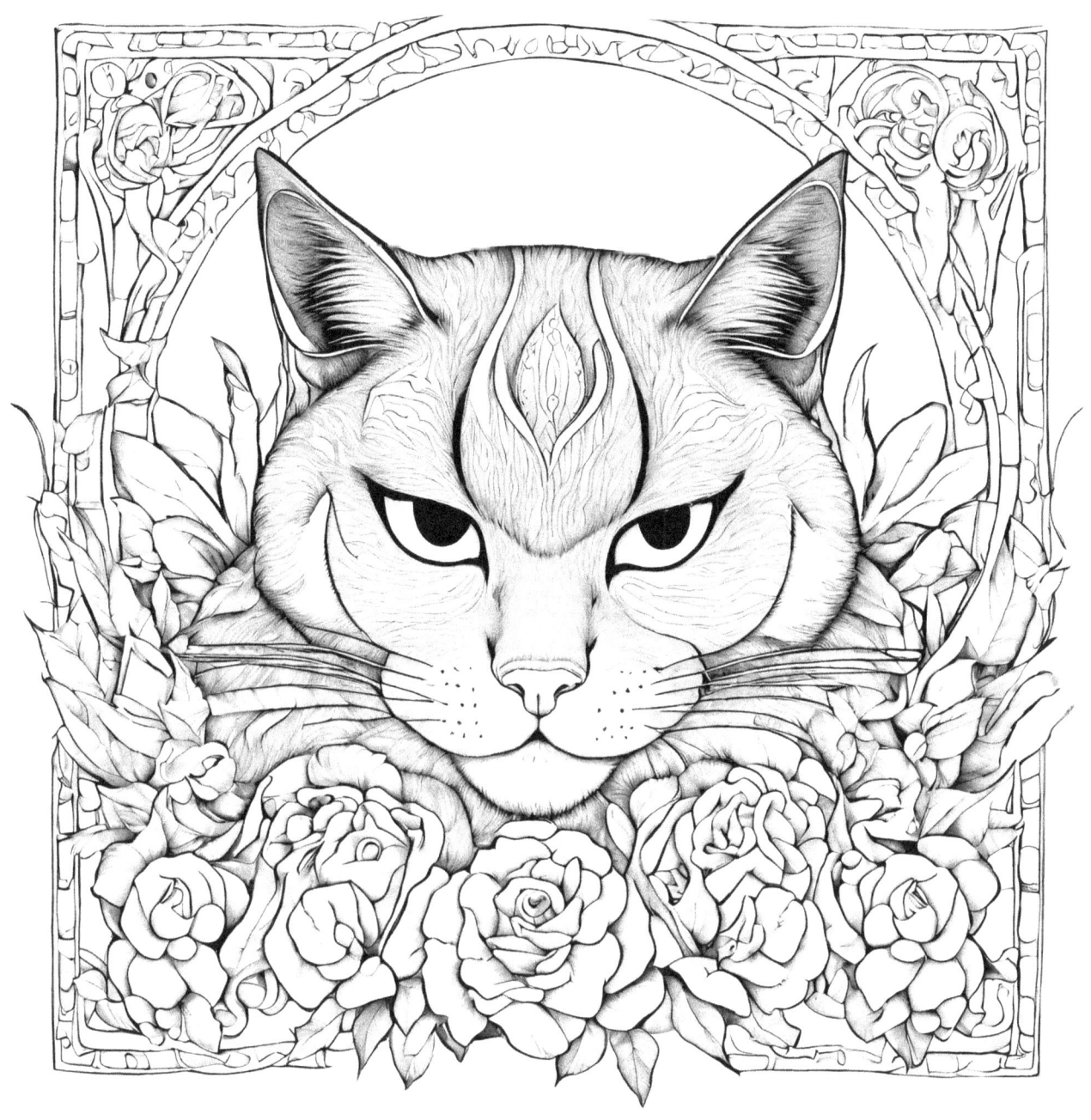

A CAT IS A LION IN A JUNGLE OF SMALL BUSHES.

INDIAN PROVERB

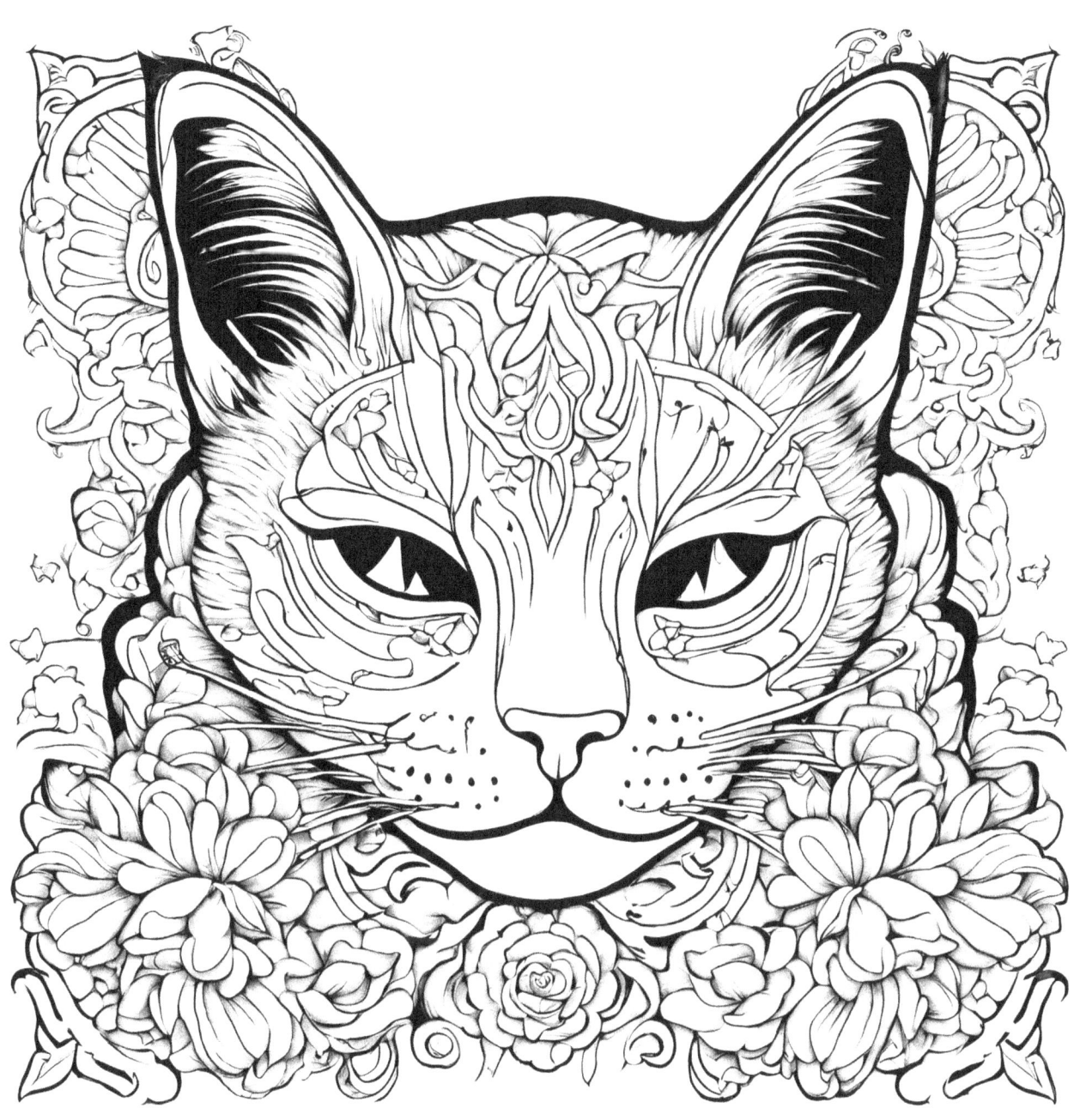

PERHAPS ONE REASON WE ARE FASCINATED BY CATS IS BECAUSE SUCH A SMALL ANIMAL CAN CONTAIN SO MUCH INDEPENDENCE, DIGNITY AND FREEDOM OF SPIRIT. UNLIKE THE DOG, THE CAT´S PERSONALITY IS NEVER BET ON A HUMAN´S. HE DEMANDS ACCEPTANCE ON HIS OWN TERMS.

LLOYD ALEXANDER

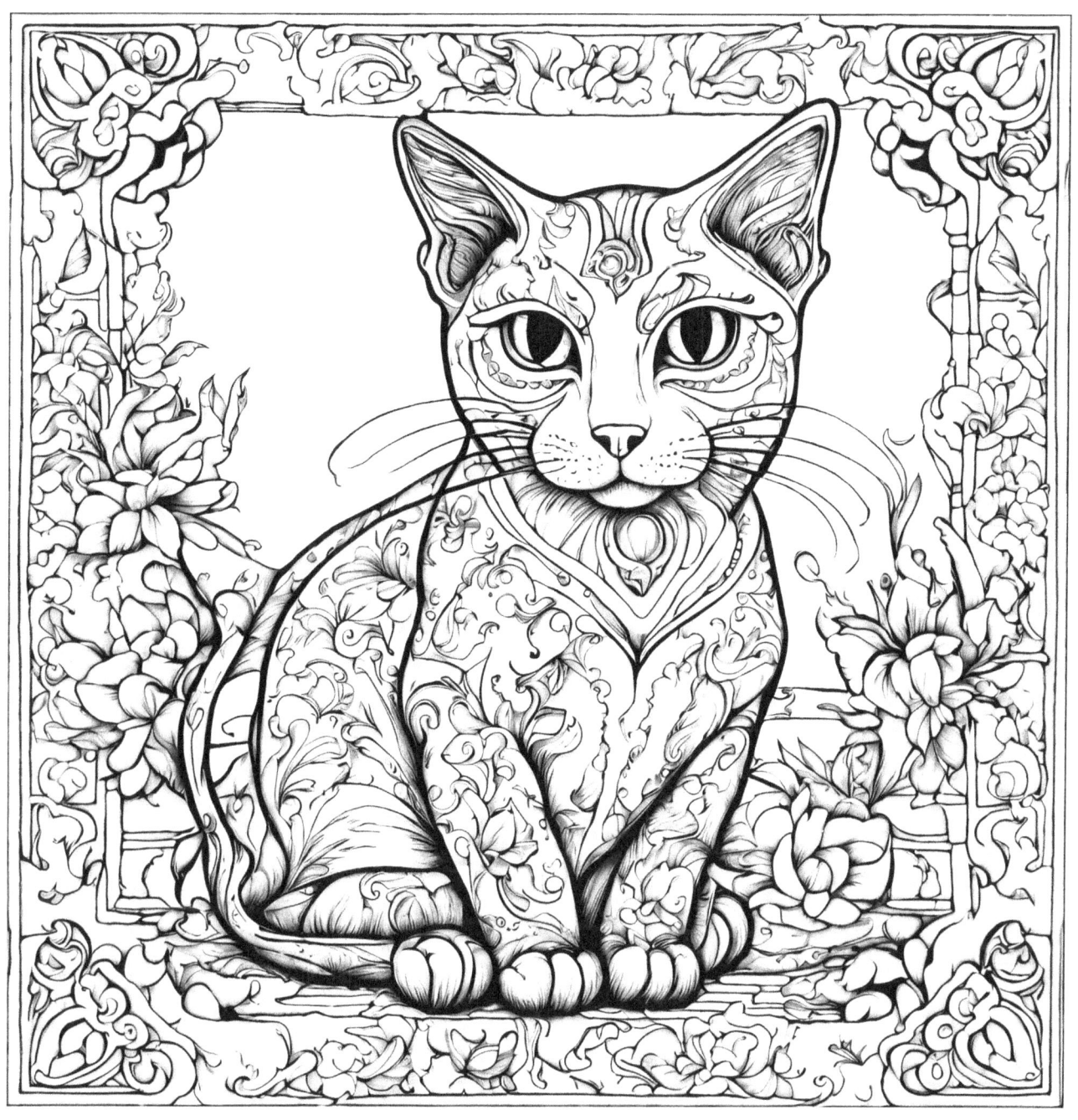

TIME SPENT WITH CATS IS NEVER WASTED

SIGMUND FREUD

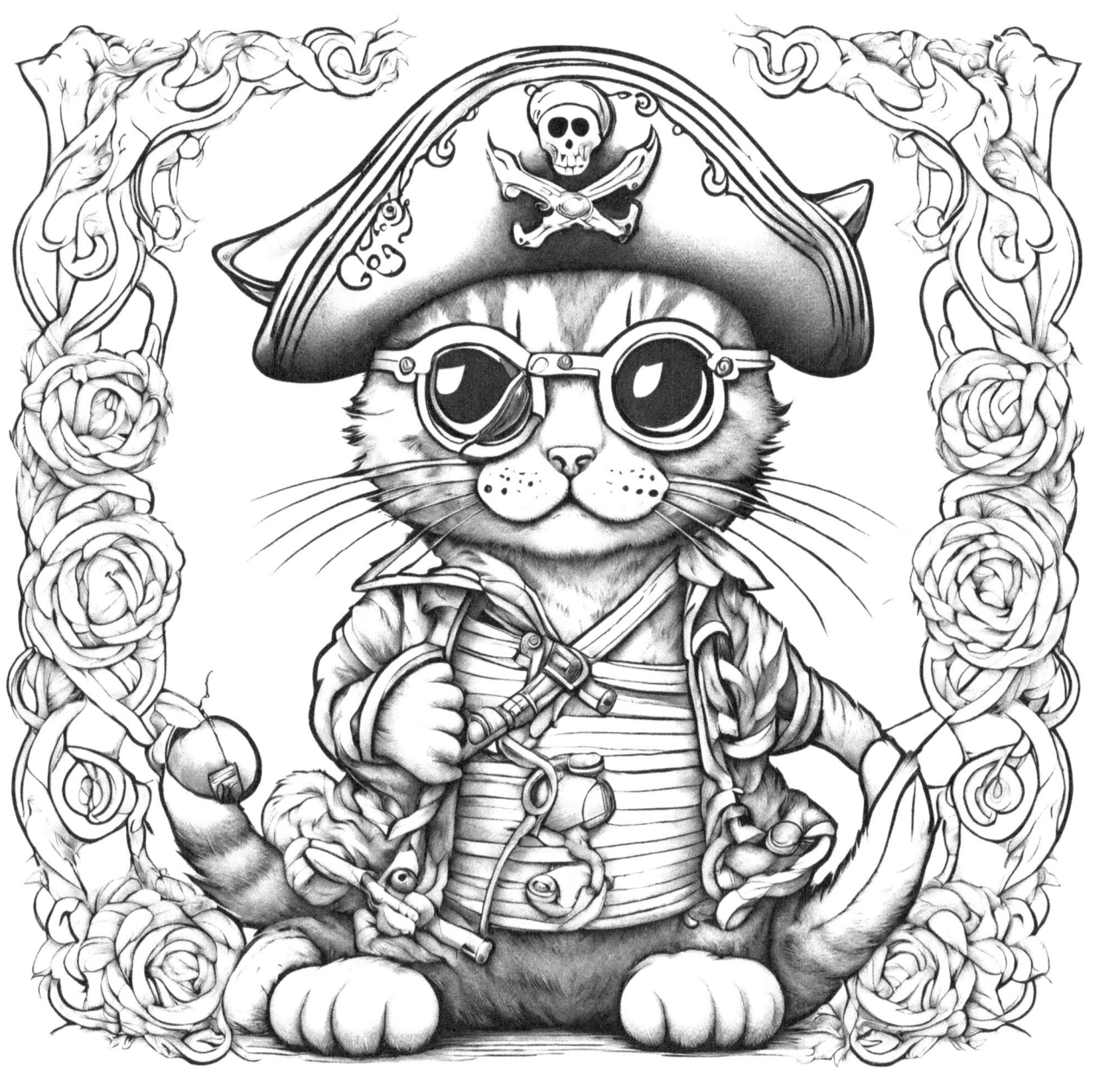

CATS KNOW HOW TO OBTAIN FOOD WITHOUT LABOR, SHELTER WITHOUT CONFINEMENT, AND LOVE WITHOUT PENALTIES.

W.L.GEORGE

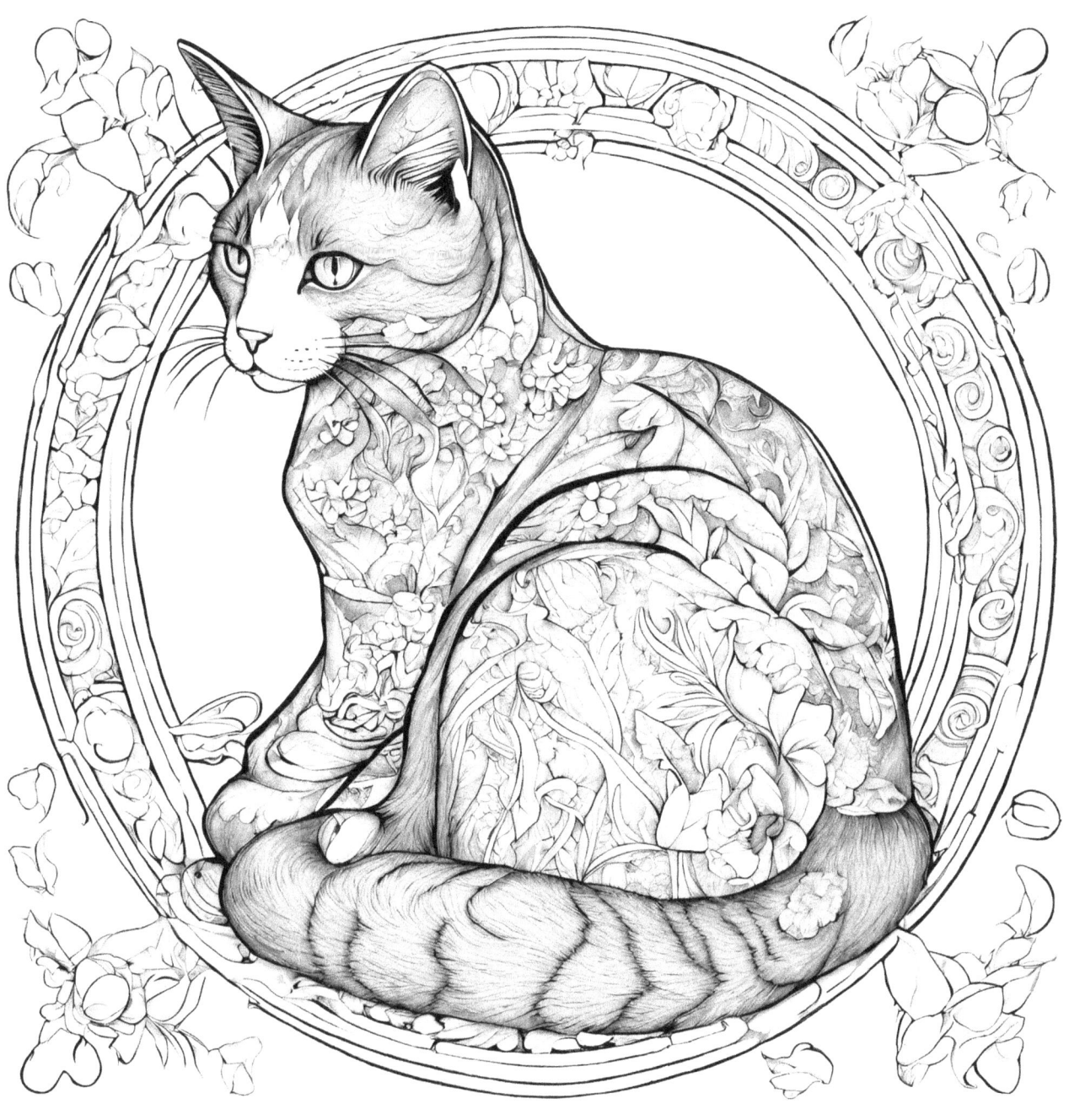

A CAT WILL DO WHAT IT WANTS WHEN IT WANTS, AND THERE'S NOT A THING YOU CAN DO ABOUT IT.

FRANK PERKINS

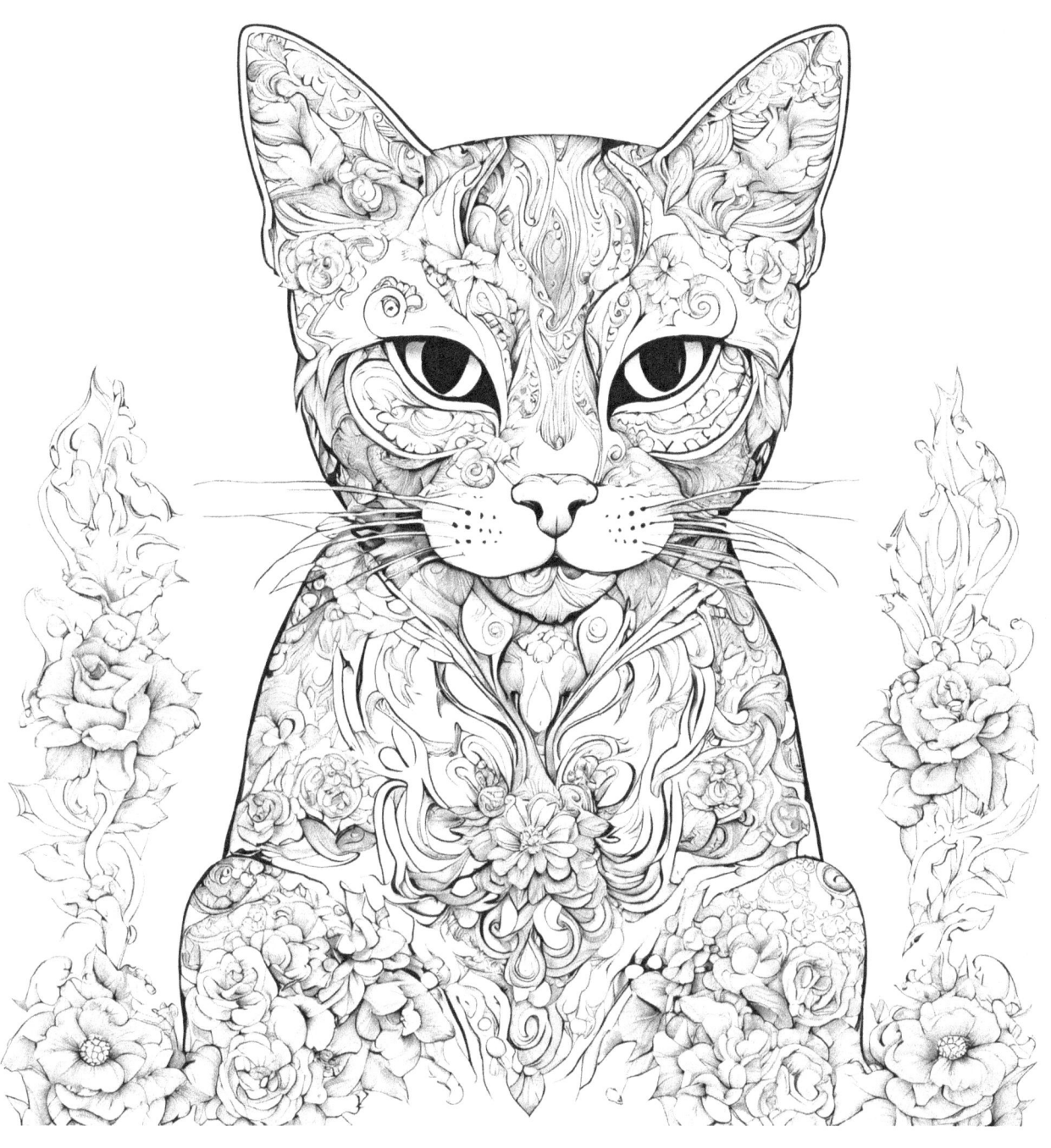

CATS ARE THE ULTIMATE NARCISSISTS. YOU CAN TELL THIS BY ALL THE TIME THEY SPEND GROOMING THEMSELVES.

JAMES GORMAN

www.ingramcontent.com/pod-product-compliance
Lightning Source LLC
Chambersburg PA
CBHW082151290526
45794CB00008B/3256